THE EXPERIENCE OF NO-SELF

THE EXPERIENCE OF NO-SELF

A Contemplative Journey

Bernadette Roberts

SHAMBHALA
Boulder & London 1984

SHAMBHALA PUBLICATIONS, INC.
Boulder, Colorado 80306-0271

First Shambhala edition
Distributed in the United States by Random House
and in Canada by Random House of Canada Ltd.

Printed in the United States of America

Library of Congress Cataloging in Publication Data
Roberts, Bernadette, 1931-
    The experience of no-self.
    Reprint. Originally published: Sunspot, N.M.:
Iroquois House, 1982.
    1. Contemplation—Case studies.   2. Depersonalization—
Religious aspects—Christianity—Case studies.   3. Roberts,
Bernadette, 1931-   4. Catholics—United States—
Biography.   I. Title.
BV5091.C7R6 1984   248.2'2'0924 [B]   84-5500
ISBN 0-87773-289-2 (pbk.)
ISBN 0-394-72693-6 (Random House: pbk.)

"To contemplatives East and West —especially those who dwell on the spiritual mountains of Carmel and New Camaldoli"

Contents

Introduction

This is the personal account of a two-year journey during which I experienced the falling away of everything I can
call a self. It was a journey through an unknown passageway that led to a life so new and different that, despite forty
years of varied contemplative experiences, I never suspected
its existence. Because it was beyond my expectations, the
experience of no-self remained incomprehensible in terms of
any frame of reference known to me and, though I searched
the libraries and bookstores, I did not find there an explanation or an account of a similar journey which, at the time,
would have been clarifying and most helpful. Owing then to
the deficiency of recorded accounts, I have written these
pages, trusting that they may be of use to those who share
the destiny of making this journey beyond the self.

Though my contemplative experiences began at an
early age, it was not until I was fifteen that I discovered how
these experiences fit like the inset of a child's puzzle into the
larger framework of the Christian contemplative tradition.
This finding was followed by ten years of relative seclusion
in order to pursue the Christian goal of union with God,
and once I had the certitude of this goal's realization, I
entered the more ordinary stream of life where I remain to
this day.

Within the traditional framework, the Christian notion of loss-of-self is generally regarded as a transformation

of the ego or lower self into the true or higher self as it approaches union with God; throughout this journey, however, the self retains its individual uniqueness and never loses its ontological sense of personal selfhood. Thus, the notion I maintained of being lost to myself meant, at the same time, being found in God as the sharer of a divine life. It meant a permanent state in which God, the "still-point" at the center of being, was ever accessible to the contemplative gaze — a point from which the life of the self arises and into which it sometimes disappears. But this latter experience of loss-of-self is only transient. It does not constitute a permanent state, nor did it occur to me that it could ever do so.

Prior to this journey, I had given little thought to the self, its perimeters or definitions. I took for granted the self was the totality of being, body and soul, mind and feelings; a being centered around God, its power-axis and still-point. Thus, because the self at its deepest center is a run-on with the divine, I never found any true self apart from God, for to find the One, is to find the other.

Because this was the limit of my expectations (and my experiences), I was all the more surprised and bewildered when I came upon a permanent state in which there was no self, not even a higher self, a true self, or anything that could be called a self. Clearly, I had fallen outside my own, as well as the traditional, frame of reference when I came upon a path that seemed to begin where the writers on the contemplative life had left off. But with the clear certitude of the self's disappearance, there automatically arose the question of what had fallen away — what was the self? What, exactly, had it been? Then too, there was the all-important question: what remained in its absence? This journey was the gradual revelation of the answers to these questions, answers that had to be derived solely from personal experience since no outside explanation was forthcoming.

With the exception of the little I could find by Meister Eckhart, I was left without a way to account for this experience, and even when I turned to books in the Eastern traditions, I encountered the same deficit of accounts — at least accounts that were available to me through the local channels. Though the Buddhist notion of no-self struck me as true, its failure to acknowledge, or first come upon the wholeness of the self in its union with God, naturally left the Christian experience of no-self unaccounted for. Quite possibly, the extent to which the individual first discovers this union is the extent to which its falling away will appear all the more inexplicable and bewildering. It is only when this transition is over, or when we have become acclimated to a new life, that the relative difference between self and no-self recedes beyond reach; but by this time, we have already seen what is down the road and the need for clarification no longer exists.

Realizing then, that I was alone in this gap between the ultimate Christian notion of loss-of-self and its immediate experience, I came to a few conclusions of my own. In main, I am convinced that the contemplative life is composed of two distinct and separate movements, well marked and defined by the nature of their experiences alone. The first movement is toward self's union with God which runs parallel with the psychological process of integration, wherein the emphasis is on interior trials and dark nights by which the self is established in a permanent union with God — the still-point and axis of its being. In this process we discover that the self is not lost; rather a new self has been found that now functions as an undivided unit from its deepest, innermost center.

Following this first movement is an interval (twenty years in my case) during which this union is tested by a variety of exterior trials whereby this oneness is revealed in all its enduring depths of stability and toughness against all forces that would move, fragment, or disturb its center; thus, it is a period of discovering the beauty, the intense wonder of this gratuitous union and, above all, of discovering what this wholeness means and how it works in our daily lives. Then, too, it is a period of becoming acclimated to the relative difference between life with the old, easily fragmented self, and life with a new self that cannot be moved from its center in God. Still more, this seems to be a stage in which, if exterior trials are not forthcoming, the contemplative may seek them because the energy created by this union must move outward (as a unit and not as a scattered force) to find expression, to accept challenge — even suffering — as a way to both reveal and affirm this enduring love.

I might add that these intervening years between movements are also largely ignored in contemplative literature; their importance is highly underestimated due to the failure to realize that this interval is actually the preparation for a great explosion — a quiet one, however — that ushers in another major turning-point. It seems that at the end of this period a point is reached where the self is so completely aligned with the still-point it can no longer be moved, even in its first movements, from this center. It can no longer be tested by any force or trial, nor moved by the winds of change, and at this point the self has obviously outworn its function; it is no longer needed or useful and life can go on without it. We are ready to move on, to go beyond the self, beyond even its most intimate union with God, and this is where we enter yet another new life — a life best categorized, perhaps, as a life without a self.

The onset of this second movement is characerized by the falling away of the self and a coming upon of "that" which remains when it is gone. But this going-out is an upheaval, a complete turnabout of such proportions it cannot possibly be missed, under-emphasized, or sufficiently stressed as a major landmark in the contemplative life. It is far more than the discovery of life without a self. The immediate, inevitable result is a change of consciousness, an emergence into a new way of knowing that entails a tremendous readjustment when the self can no longer be an object of awareness. The reflexive mechanism of the mind — or whatever it is that allows us to be self-conscious — is cut off or permanently suspended so the mind is ever after held in a fixed now-moment, out of which it cannot move in its uninterrupted gaze upon the Unknown.

This journey then, is nothing more, yet nothing less, than a period of acclimating to a new way of seeing; a time of transition and revelation as it gradually comes upon "that" which remains when there is no self. This is not a journey for those who expect love and bliss; rather, it is for the hardy who have been tried in fire and have come to rest in the tough, immovable trust in "that" which lies beyond the known, beyond the self, beyond union, and even beyond love and trust itself.

Since the moment self-consciousness comes to a permanent end — and the journey begins — is such a decisive stroke or milestone in the contemplative life, I can only speculate why so little has been said of this breakthrough; in fact, I may never get over the silence on the part of writers who say nothing about this second movement. Perhaps some contemplatives take in stride what to others is a monumental explosion; or possibly, writers downplay what they do not understand or deem unorthodox or rare; or perhaps — and this is my view — they have confused these two movements by failing to adequately distinguish between them: that is, to distinguish between two different changes in consciousness; between going beyond the lower (ego) self, and later, the higher Self; between union with God, and the identity of God. Since viewed as a whole, the contemplative life is on a single continuum, it is often difficult to draw a line and see clear distinctions until one has personally encountered these landmarks, at which time the difference between these movements becomes obvious and unmistakable.

My purpose then, in writing this account, is to help clarify the second movement, to make it more recognizable

and to bring to light, if possible, the ultimate, final realization of the Christian notion of loss-of-self. In part, this attempt stems from the conviction that this movement is not
unusual and that many individuals have come, or will
come, to this stage wherein some clarifications will be as relevant to them as they would have been to me. Though no
two will have the same experiences, I feel sure that for those
who had found their true self in God and then lost it, there
will be certain consequences and findings in common.

While the journey was in progress, I tried to write of its
events, but it was not until it was over — or until the relative difference between life with or without a self was no
longer apparent — that I wrote the account in its present
form and gave it to several friends for their comments and
criticisms. Though much too generous to cite me for either
its content or its homely narrative, they were nevertheless
honest with their questions and objections. In response to
these, I wrote Part II, trying to find the answers I didn't
have.

In writing these final chapters I learned more about the
journey than I learned while it was in progress. It seems that
the nature of this passage is a total state of unknowing
which, while it lent a certain beauty and air of mystery to its
unfoldment, also lent a sense of bewilderment which was responsible, I believe, for certain hardships — hardships that
might have been avoided if some explanation had been forthcoming. It was only when the journey was over, and I could
view it in retrospect, that I came to a better understanding
and was able, therefore, to offer the explanations given in
the final chapters.

Here too, I have made reference to my earlier background where it seemed necessary for understanding the
present journey in its relationship to the past. This background was not given at the outset because my present concern focuses solely on the relatively unexplored dimension
of life — this movement beyond the self. Also, I knew that

if I did not record this transition as soon as possible, it would soon be forgotten, because one of the first lessons learned on this journey is that the passing of each experience leaves nothing in its wake, hardly a footprint and certainly not a vivid memory. In a word, one learns to live without a past.

For this reason, I wrote quickly before the journey became lost forever and life without a self grew as dim as the day of my birth. But at the same time, release from the past has made it possible to write on a personal level — something I would not have dared to undertake prior to this time — because the journey no longer belongs to "me." I look upon it as I do any other fact of life or event taking place around us. Thus, it now stands unalterably by itself where it remains forever — but a thing of the past.

In conclusion, I must re-emphasize that the following experiences do not belong to the first contemplative movement or the soul's establishment in a state of union with God. I have written elsewhere of this first journey and feel that enough has been said of it already, since this movement is inevitably the exclusive concern of contemplative writers. Thus it is only where these writers leave off that I propose to begin. Here now, begins the journey beyond union, beyond self and God, a journey into the silent and still regions of the Unknown.

Part I   The Journey

Chapter 1

Through past experience I had become familiar with many different types and levels of silence. There is a silence within; a silence that descends from without; a silence that stills existence; and a silence that engulfs the entire universe. There is a silence of the self and its faculties of will, thought, memory, and emotions. There is a silence in which there is nothing, a silence in which there is something; and finally, there is the silence of no-self and the silence of God. If there was any path on which I could chart my contemplative experiences, it would be this ever-expanding and deepening path of silence.

On one occasion, however, this path seemed to come to an end, when I entered a silence from which I would never totally emerge. But I must preface this account by saying that on previous occasions, I had come upon a pervasive silence of the faculties so total as to give rise to subtle apprehensions of fear. It was a fear of being engulfed forever, of being lost, annihilated, or blacking out and, possibly, never returning. In such moments, to ward off the fear, I would make some movement of abandoning my fate to God — a gesture of the will, a thought, some type of projection. And every time I did this, the silence would be broken and I would gradually return to my usual self — and security. Then, one day, this was not to be the case.

Down the road from where I lived there was a monas-

tery by the sea, and on afternoons when I could get away, I
liked to spend some time alone in the silence of its chapel.
This particular afternoon was no different from others.
Once again there was a pervasive silence and once again I
waited for the onset of fear to break it up. But this time the
fear never came. Whether by habit of expectation or the
reality of a fear held in abeyance, I felt some moments of
suspense or tension — as if waiting for fear to touch me.
During these moments of waiting, I felt as if I were poised
on a precipice or balanced on a thin tightrope, with the
known (myself) on one side and the unknown (God) on the
other. A movement of fear would have been a movement
toward the self and the known. Would I pass over this time,
or would I fall back into my self — as usual? Since there was
no power of my own to move or choose, I knew the deci-
sion was not mine; within, all was still, silent and motionless. In the stillness, I was not aware of the moment when
the fear and tension of waiting had left. Still, I continued to
wait for a movement not of myself and when no movement
came, I simply remained in a great stillness.

Sister was rattling the keys of the chapel door. It was
time to lock up, and time to go home and prepare dinner for
my children. Always in the past, having to abruptly pull out
of a deep silence was difficult, for my energies were then at a
low ebb, and the effort of moving was like lifting a dead
weight. This time, however, it suddenly occurred to me not
to think about getting up, but to just *do* it. I think I learned
a valuable lesson here, because I left the chapel as a feather
floats in the wind. Once outside, I fully expected to return
to my ordinary energies and thinking mind, but this day I
had a difficult time because I was continually falling back
into the great silence. The drive home was a constant battle
against complete unconsciousness, and trying to get dinner
was like trying to move a mountain.

For three exhausting days, it was a battle to stay awake
and ward off the silence that every second threatened to

overpower me. The only way I could accomplish the minimum of chores was by persistently reminding myself of what I was doing: now I'm peeling the carrots, now I'm cutting them, now I'm getting out a pan, now I'm putting water in the pan and on and on until, finally, I was so exhausted I would have to run for the couch. The moment I lay down I immediately blacked out. Sometimes it seemed I was out for hours, when it was only five minutes; at other times, it seemed like five minutes when it was hours. In this blackout there were no dreams, no awareness of my surroundings, no thoughts, no experiences — absolutely nothing.

On the fourth day, I noticed the silence easing up so I could stay awake with less effort and, therefore, I trusted myself to go shopping for groceries. I do not know what happened, but suddenly a lady was shaking me and asking, "Are you asleep?" I smiled at her while trying to get my bearings because, for the moment, I had not the slightest idea how I got in the store or what I should be doing. So I had to start all over again: now I am pushing the basket, now I must get some oranges, and so on. The morning of the fifth day, I could not find my slippers anywhere, but when getting breakfast for the children, I opened the refrigerator and what I found there was unbelievable, positively ludicrous.

By the ninth day, the silence had so eased up I felt assured that a little while longer and all would be normal again. But as the days went by, and I was once more able to function as usual, I noticed something was missing and I couldn't put my finger on it. Something, or some part of me had not returned. Some part of me was still in silence. It was as if some part of my mind had closed down. I blamed it on the memory because it was the last to return, and when it finally did, I noticed how flat and lifeless it was — like colorless slides on an antique film. It was dead. Not only was the distant past empty, but also the past of the previous minutes.

Now when something is dead you soon lose the habit of trying to resurrect it; thus, when the memory is lifeless, you learn to live as one who has no past — you learn to live in the present moment. That this could now be done effortlessly — and out of sheer necessity — was one good outcome of an otherwise exhausting experience. And even when I regained my practical memory, the effortless living in the present never left. But with the return of a practical memory, I discounted my earlier notion of what was missing and decided that the silent aspect of my mind was actually a kind of "absorption," an absorption in the unknown, which for me of course, was God. It was like a continuous gaze at the great, silent Unknowable which no activity could interrupt. This was another welcomed outcome of the initial experience.

This interpretation of the silent aspect of my mind (absorption) seemed sufficiently explanatory for about a month, when I again changed my mind and decided that this absorption was actually an awareness, a special kind of "seeing" so that what had really happened was not a closedown of any kind, but actually an opening-up — nothing was missing, "something" had been added. After awhile, however, this notion also did not seem to fit; it was somehow dissatisfying; something else had happened, so I decided to go to the library to see if I could solve this mystery through someone else's experience.

What I found out is that, if it cannot be found in the works of John of the Cross, it will probably not be found at all. While the writings of the Saint were well known to me, I could not find there an explanation of my specific experience; nor was I able to find it anywhere in the library. But it was coming home that day, walking downhill with a panorama of valley and hills before me, that I turned my gaze inward, and what I saw, stopped me in my tracks. Instead of the usual unlocalized center of myself, there was nothing there; it was empty; and at the moment of seeing this there

was a flood of quiet joy and I knew, finally I knew what
was missing — it was my "self."

Physically, I felt as if a great burden had been lifted
from me; I felt so light I looked down at my feet to be sure
they were on the ground. Later I thought of St. Paul's experience, "Now, not I, but Christ lives in me," and realized
that despite my emptiness, no one else had moved in to take
my place; so I decided that Christ WAS the joy, the emptiness itself; He was all that was left of this human experience.
For days I walked with this joy that, at times, was so great, I
marveled at the flood gates and wondered how long they
would hold.

For me, this experience was the height of my contemplative vocation. It was the ending of a question that had
plagued me for years: where do "I" leave off and God begin?
Over the years, the line that separated us had grown so thin
and faded that most of the time I couldn't see it anymore,
but always my mind had wanted desperately to know: what
was His and what was mine? Now my quandary was over.
There was no "mine" anymore, there was only His. I could
have lived in this joyous state the rest of my life, but such
was not in the Great Plan. It was just a matter of days, a
week perhaps, when my entire spiritual life — the work, the
suffering, the experiences, and the goals of a lifetime — suddenly exploded into a million irretrievable pieces and there
was nothing, absolutely nothing left.

Chapter 2

When the joy of my own emptiness began to wane, I decided to rejuvenate it by spending some solitary time gazing into my empty self. Though the center of self was gone, I was sure the remaining emptiness, the silence and joy, was God Himself.

Thus, on one occasion, with full hedonistic deliberation, I settled myself down and turned my gaze inward. Almost immediately the empty space began to expand, and expanded so rapidly it seemed to explode; then, in the pit of my stomach I had the feeling of falling a hundred floors in a non-stop elevator, and in this fall every sense of life was drained from me. The moment of landing, I know: *When there is no personal self, there is also no personal God.* I saw clearly how the two go together — and where they went, I have never found out.

For a while I sat there mentally and emotionally stunned. I couldn't think about what had happened, nor was there any response in me at all. Around me there was only stillness, and in this complete stillness I waited and waited for some kind of reaction to set in, or something to happen next, but nothing ever did. In me there was no sense of life, no movement and no feeling; finally I realized I no longer had a "within" at all.

The moment of falling had been such a complete wipeout that never again would I have any sense of possessing a life I could call my own — or any other type of life. My interior or spiritual life was finished. There was no more gazing within; from now on my eyes could only look outward. At the time, I had no way of knowing the tremendous repercussions that would follow this sudden event. I had to learn bit by bit; on a totally experiential level, because my mind could not comprehend what had happened since this event and everything that followed fell outside any frame of reference known to me. From here on, I literally had to grope my way along an unknown path.

My first thought was: oh, no, not another Dark Night! I was accustomed to those experiential disappearances of God and was rather disappointed to think there were any of them left. But when none of the usual reactions set in (anything from anxiety to agony — you name it), I felt this experience fell outside anything John of the Cross had described, and put the notion out of my mind. Besides, it didn't make any difference; I simply had to cope with the reality of the here and now, a reality in which there was no sense of life in me.

So I sat there fully awake, healthy, faculties unimpaired, obviously alive; in a word, all systems were functioning as usual — but I felt no life. What do you do now? I decided I might as well get an early start preparing dinner, but as I did so, all the usual movements now seemed so mechanical I felt I had suddenly become a robot, for I could no longer endow my work with any personal energies. I did my chores with no life to back them up and they were all totally mechanical — a mere conditioned habit of movement.

After a while this "gets" to you and you gradually have a pressing need to find some life somewhere. Hoping to find it, I went into the garden and stood there looking around. I knew there was life there, but I couldn't feel it, so I went around like a blind man, touching everything: the leaves and flowers; reaching up I grabbed the pine branches and let them slide through my hands; stooping down, I ran my hands through the soil. Then I lay down on the grass, palms downward, looking up through the branches of the pine tree and felt the moving air flow over me. It was good to be there; everything was okay. Somewhere there was life all around me, even if there was no life in me.

Later that evening before the sun went down, I took myself to a place I always went in time of crisis — the local bird refuge. It was only a few blocks from home, and the route offered beautiful vistas of the sea with its miles of shoreline and hills that rose up behind the refuge. Usually I only climbed in a little way. Beyond the stump where I would sit was a marsh that grew deeper with mud and water as it approached one of the ponds formed by the river which emptied into the sea. But this day, I took off my shoes and socks and climbed into the middle of the refuge until I found a small rock barely visible above the mud. Here, among the tall reeds and wild grasses I sat down and disappeared — literally sank into the life that was around me, and soon, on me as well.

Always I had felt at home here. It was a place of great peace and a mysterious stillness. By experience I knew that thinking would never solve the problems of life; it was just being here, out-of-doors, in the midst of real life, that automatically separated the relevant from the irrelevant, so that upon returning home, all the irrelevancies had been swept away and I could see clearly the path I must go. So too, on this particular day, I knew I was home, more at home perhaps than ever before. Around the little rock, life was teeming and overflowing, it was everywhere, and so compensated for my own lack of life that the earlier events of the day seemed not to have happened. For sure, this was where I belonged, surrounded and locked securely into this elusive unlocalized thing called "life." After all, I thought, perhaps no man is better than the elements of which he is composed, for these elements are his very life — but how this could be so, I did not know. Just to be there was all that mattered.

The next weeks were spent mainly out-of-doors. Life indoors had become almost intolerable because it was now so routine, lifeless, and devoid of personal energies that it was all I could do to accomplish the minimum of chores. But out-of-doors somewhere life was flowing — peaceful, forgetful, unknowable — and this was where I had to be. So I roamed the hills, the riverbanks and the seashore just looking, watching, and being there.

Though I had looked and watched all my life, this time was different because I could not more find life in the trees, the wild flowers, or the waters than I could find it in myself; and yet, there was life all around us. It's strange how the mind wants to localize and pinpoint this unknowable thing called life, and when its demands are met, it goes blind with this knowledge and is forever locked out of the only true security man has — or so I would soon learn. For now, however, I was looking for this security and could not find it. Though everything seemed as empty as myself I knew there was life somewhere in nature, and for now, I wanted only to be there and be a part of it.

On a bluff above the sea, overlooking a cove of rocks on which the seals would doze, there stood a gnarled, wind-blown cypress tree, a favorite spot of mine — until a Forest Ranger one day told me to leave, lest I add to the soil erosion. Between the tortured roots, which allowed for no other growth, there was a place to sit down without mashing a single dandelion or disturbing the varied flora that made this bluff so beautiful.

It was here that nature finally yielded its secret to me in a simple, still moment in which I saw how it all worked. God or life was not *in* anything. It was just the reverse; everything was *in* God. And we were not in God like drops of water that could be separated from the sea, but more like ...well, the only thing I could think of was the notion of trying to pinch out a spot on an inflated balloon; if you pinch out a spot and try to cut it off, the whole thing will pop because it can't be done. You can't separate anything from God, for as soon as you let go of the notion of separateness, everything falls back into the wholeness of God and life.

But to see how this works and to explain it are two different matters. One thing is for sure: as long as we are caught up in words, definitions, and all that the mind wants to cling to, we can never see how it works. And until we can go beyond our notions regarding the true nature of life, we will never realize how totally secure we really are, and how all the fighting for individual survival and self-security is a waste of energy.

This insight then, opened a new door for me. I began to see things differently and, above all, I quit wandering around looking for life — obviously it's everywhere; we're in it, and it's all there is.

Solely in retrospect, I would like to mention a certain lesson learned on this journey. I learned that a single insight is not sufficient to bring about any real change. In time, every insight has a way of filtering down to our usual frame of reference, and once we make it fit, it gets lost in the milieu of the mind; the mind which has a tendency to pollute every insight. The secret of allowing an insight to become a permanent way of knowing and seeing is not to touch it, cling to it, dogmatize it, or even to think about it. Insights come and go, but to have them stay, we have to flow with them; otherwise, no change is possible. It's a mistake to think that because we've been thrown the ball, we know in which direction to run. Perhaps our greatest insights are lost this way: we plunk them down in our usual frame of reference and go nowhere. But if we're really ready when the ball comes, the sheer momentum will carry us and place us in the flow — wherever it is going. Now I pass this along only because I had to learn this the hard way, for when the pieces didn't fit, or when an insight fell outside my frame of reference, I felt more lost than was really necessary. I could have saved myself a lot of trouble, looking and searching for my own unanswerable questions.

An example of learning the hard way occurred here, with the falling away of all feeling of possessing individual life, which forced me to look for life outside myself. Since I had already lived some forty years, experiencing life within, this was a very difficult time — a time of transition and acclimation without being able to see ahead or understanding what had happened. Nevertheless, I did the best I could to help myself, and since I was a daily communicant, it occurred to me it might be of some avail to carry the Eucharist with me at all times — in a pix around my neck. With the falling away of life within, the reception of the Eucharist no longer had any effect on me. Where before, it had always drawn me into its mysterious silence, now, no such change occurred; if anything, there was too much silence. Thus, with the failure of the Eucharist to restore a sense of life within, I felt doubly lost and decided I might at least carry it with me in my search to find God without.

After a few weeks, however, I saw this ruse was not working when it brought no sense of life or security, nor brought about any change in the situation. Then, under the cypress tree on the day already mentioned, I consumed the host and saw all things were *in* God, that he was closer and more personal than I had ever dared to expect. To suddenly realize you live and walk in God is a unique discovery that forever dispels the sense of loss that ensues when the feeling of a personal life falls away.

If nothing else, this incident (and many that remain untold) attests to the continual effort to cling to the usual frame of reference, a clinging that revealed nothing until the hold had been released. I might add that among the many notions that had to be abandoned was my notion of abandonment itself. It was not I, who had abandoned the self to God, rather it was God who had abandoned the self completely; and that once beyond the self, everything goes, even "that" which I had expected would remain.

A week or two after the above insight, I was making a retreat with the Hermit Monks on the Big Sur. About the second day, toward late afternoon, I was standing on their windy hillside looking down over the ocean when a seagull came into view, gliding, dipping, playing with the wind. I watched it as I'd never watched anything before in my life. I almost seemed to be mesmerized; it was as if I was watching myself flying, for there was not the usual division between us. Yet, something more was there than just a lack of separateness, "something" truly beautiful and unknowable. Finally I turned my eyes to the pine-covered hills behind the monastery and still, there was no division, only something "there" that was flowing with and through every vista and particular object of vision. To see the Oneness of everything is like having special 3D glasses put before your eyes; I thought to myself: for sure, this is what they mean when they say "God IS everywhere."

I could have stood there looking for the rest of my life, but after a while, I thought it was all too good to be true; it was some hoax of the mind and when the bell rang, it would all disappear. Well, the bell finally rang, and it rang the next day and for the rest of the week, but the 3D glasses were still intact. What I had taken as a trick of the mind was to become a permanent way of seeing and knowing which I will do my best to describe as my whole world turned slowly inside-out. I was never to revert back to the usual relative way of seeing separateness or individuality; but make no mistake, the obliteration of separateness is meaningless in itself. What is important about this way of seeing is THAT into which all separateness dissolves.

Before going further and attempting to describe this new way of seeing, I would like to say that after discovering God was everywhere — or His Oneness, as I called it — I was compensated a thousandfold for the bewildering loss of a personal God within. It seems I had first to move through the personal and then through the impersonal before I realized God was closer than either, and beyond them both.

The notions and the experiences of God as being personally within or impersonally without, are purely relative experiences, pertaining to the self and its particular type of consciousness. God, however, is beyond the relativity of our minds and experiences; indeed, he is so close he can never be localized. But to realize this closeness — to see it — is to discover that God is everywhere, and at the same time, to see how he is all that exists — because wherever we look there is nothing else to see. In truth then, God is neither personal nor impersonal, neither within nor without, but is everywhere in general and nowhere in particular. Simply put: God is all that Is — all, of course, but the self.

Chapter 3

Eventually it became imperative to make some changes in my lifestyle. For the time being at least, it had become impossible to feel at one with the constant flow of irrelevancies and noise that made up my usual environment. Having been robbed of the energies necessary to dominate, control, and stay on top of the frequent chaotic conditions in the home, my effectiveness as a mother to four teenagers dropped sharply to zero. When self is no longer running the show, the usual defense-mechanisms can no longer be activated, and the burden of coping falls squarely upon the energies of the physical body alone. While I never had the feeling of being nervous, upset, anxious and all that, I nevertheless had the impression that if I were to continue the same pattern of living I would be expected, from now on, to lift dead weights; and I couldn't do it.

Until the rug (my 'self') had been pulled out from under me, I never realized how utterly dependent I was upon getting around under my own steam — steam of the mind and emotions, that is, not physical steam. It seems we possess an endless array of subtle energies we don't know we have until they are gone — although later, I was to see clearly how these energies are, in fact, the self's defenses against its own annihilation. Right now, however, it was taking a long time to learn how to survive without any energy I could call my own. Learning to live this way was like learning to live all over again, and though I now understand it in retrospect, at the time I was as bewildered and groping as a man who has suddenly lost the power of his limbs.

What I seemed to need were great blocks of time for uninterrupted silence and contact with nature, because it was only in such a milieu I felt at home and at one with the flow of life. What I eventually did was pack up the camping gear and head for the forests of the high Sierras where I camped for five months, or until the snows came and I had to come down.

I went to the mountains to learn how to live a new type of existence, an existence without time, without thought, without the emotions, feelings, and energies of the self. I hadn't the slightest idea how things would go; all I knew was that I had to go and find out. While the discoveries were numerous and I have much to say about this adventure, I think I can sum it up in one phrase by saying: until I went to the mountains I had never truly lived. Not for a single day in my life had I ever lived before. Without a doubt I was in the Great Flow, so totally at one with it that every notion of ecstasy, bliss, love, and joy, pale by comparison to the extraordinary simplicity, clarity, and oneness of such an existence.

There's nothing haphazard, idle, or easy-going about forest life. On the contrary, everything there is vital, fully awake, dynamic, and intelligent. It's not a free life. The Great Flow takes its own direction sweeping everything along, and whether it would go or not, is of no consequence. There's no time to step out of the flow or to take a break; in word, it is a life completely devoid of a single irrelevancy.

One of the great mysteries I hoped to solve in this mountain solitude was the answer to my question: what is it that sees this Oneness everywhere?

And to understand the question better, I am going to back up a bit to the weeks following the initial seeing on the monks' hillside.

Gradually I began to notice a shift in this seeing. Where at first it had been very nebulous and general, I soon noticed that when I visually focused in on a flower, an animal, another person, or any particular object, slowly the particularity would recede into a nebulous Oneness, so that the object's distinctness was lost to my mind. Visually of course, nothing changed, the change was merely in the type of perception itself. Until this happened, it never occurred to me how I had always taken for granted the individuality of all objects of visual perception. But now, with the imposition of the 3D glasses, it became impossible for the mind to perceive or retain any individuality when all visual objects either faded from the mind, gave way to something else, or were "seen through" — I don't know which is the best description to use. I might also add, that I do not understand the mechanism of this change in perception, yet I regard this change as one of the most significant events in the entire journey because, it not only remained as a permanent irreversible fixture of perception, but seemed to be the necessary vehicle by which I eventually came to the final "seeing."

It is truly marvelous how this works. It is a unique type of experience, but I repeat: the marvel of it isn't the loss of individuality of the object observed; rather, the marvel is *that* into which it blends and ultimately disappears. For now, I called *that* Oneness — and of course, God.

I'm always reluctant to use the word, God, because everybody seems to carry around his own stagnant images and definitions that totally cloud the ability to step outside a narrow, individual frame of reference. If we have any conception of what God is, certainly it should be changing and expanding as we ourselves grow and change. This is the very nature of our life's movement: to expand, to open up

and blossom. Like the flowers that turn completely backward to face the light, sometimes we too, must do an about-
face if we would see what Is. Since we do not know in
which direction to turn, we must wait like the flower for the
morning sun, and with no effort or resistance, be pulled in
the direction of the light. Whatever we care to call the ultimate reality, we cannot define or qualify it because the
brain is incapable of processing this kind of data; thus we
must ever look upon words as mere descriptions of a man's
experience — the nature of which we do not really know.
For myself, the opening up of everything upon which I gazed
revealed a reality that was the same throughout, be the object animate or inanimate. For this reason I called it, Oneness. That someone else would prefer a different name is all
right with me. Just the seeing of It is all that matters.

The mysterious aspect of this type of seeing was that
while I could focus on the objects around me, I could never
focus on myself. To do so would have been as impossible as
looking into my eyes without a mirror. For this reason, I felt
like an outside observer looking upon a Oneness that included everything but myself. It were as if I were not a part
of this Oneness, not even a part of the universe; in fact, I
couldn't see where I had any existence at all. Besides the
body, all that was left was just this seeing and yet, even this
did not really belong to me for it was not localized anywhere
in my mental or physical make-up, but instead, seemed to be
on top or a little above my head — toward the front and
over the forehead. Although I continued to refer to this seeing as my wonderful glasses — because of the extra dimen-
sional aspect — I was sure this seeing was actually outside
the ordinary mind and physical body as well.

While trying to figure out the nature of this seeing, I
came upon the notion of man's original consciousness, or
the type of consciousness we all have from the beginning.
As a one-time student of child development, I knew that the
infant possesses a non-relative consciousness in which there

is no distinguishing between subject (himself) and object; consequently, he has no notion of a self. Furthermore, as we all know, the infant doesn't think, for as yet there is no content in his consciousness, nor does he have anything to remember. All of us then, were born without a reflective, self-conscious type of mind which, to me, is an apt definition of "seeing." Thus, for the adult, seeing may be a kind of return to this original form of consciousness, a form that surprisingly does not seem to hamper the ordinary activities of the practical mind. Therefore, in the process of reverting back to our original consciousness, we have to learn how to live without any self-consciousness — the build-up of a lifetime perhaps — and this is not an easy journey to take. But it's exciting to think we can take it at all, and even more exciting to think of what would happen if every man could live as he was originally intended to live.

For awhile then, this idea of man's original consciousness seemed to clarify the nature of this seeing, but one day I discovered a hole in this conclusion. While there may be no self-consciousness in this seeing, the seeing alone constitutes a subject, just as the Oneness it sees, constitutes an object, for the distinction between the seeing and the Oneness was clear to me and never lent itself to any form of identity. Thus in this case, seeing (observing) is not identical with the seen (observed), which put me right back on a purely relative plane of existence — even though there is no self that does the seeing. What this means is that the infant's consciousness may actually be relative even though it is not self-reflecting. But however this works, I could never find any relationship between this seeing and Oneness because, as I have said: at all times they were totally distinct and separate.

Months later, this same question of relationship came up in a conversation, and while trying to think of an answer, the notions of original consciousness, seeing, and Oneness, seemed to float out the window and over the hillside until they finally disappeared from sight somewhere over the ocean. Thus, the question of relationship of seer and seen had no answer. But at the time of which I speak, I was still thinking up the questions, because I lived a full nine months with the wonderful glasses ever focused on the Oneness they saw everywhere, and as far as I was concerned, this was the end of the road.

Nevertheless, I still find it interesting to speculate about what the infant may actually see and know before his mind has become conditioned by his environment. At the same time we may ponder the animal's form of consciousness and the possibility that it may know and see something that man has lost in his endless battle for survival of the self. Then too, who knows what great intelligence may be locked into the very elements that compose man and the universe — an intelligence without any consciousness at all? One thing is certain: with our thinking, rational mind, we'll never come upon these answers. Our mind, limited tool that it is, is so continually taken up in the service of self that it cannot come upon that which is beyond all such concerns.

Apart from trying to identify what it was that saw this Oneness, there was still the unresolved question of what remained in the absence of self. What is this that walks and talks and is aware of the eye upon Oneness? As obvious as it was, I had no mind for such a mystery and could not come upon a single explanation. Though the identity of the Oneness was known, the identity of the eye that saw it, as well as what remained in the absence of self, could not be identified. Thus, between the Oneness, the eye, and no-self, there seemed to be no true relationship.

Ultimately I discovered that the only resolution to the many questions that arose, is time. Time means change, and in the process of change my initial questions either changed, dissolved, or were resolved in the process. I had already learned that thinking never brought about change; consequently, thinking netted me nothing when it came to resolving these questions. Though questions inevitably arose, I soon learned it was important not to give them premature answer.

In similar fashion, I learned this was also true of my experiences. I discovered that as soon as I invested any value, meaning, or purpose in them, I was losing the pearl of great price by giving them a premature closure. It was only by investing no value in an experience that I was able to find out its truth or falsity. What is false never lasts; it falls away of its own accord, while what is true remains, because truth does not come and go — it is always there. So as long as our experiences come and go and we are investing in them our own values, thoughts, and emotions, we'll never find out if there is any truth in them, for truth is what remains when there are no experiences left.

I only mention this because it was one of the lessons I learned in the mountains. I learned that without any movement, reaction, or response from within — or from the self — all experiences were becoming like water on a duck's back. It were as if I had become an outside observer on the relative apsects of life, aspects in which I participated through conditioned habit, while at the same time, I was also participating in the inexplicable reality of the flow of life — true life. It seems that beyond the self, the relativity of our experiences falls away because there is nothing within to respond, nothing to hold onto an experience in order to give it value, meaning, and so on. In this way, experiences lose their relative aspects when there is nothing to which they can be relative. This is why, when there is no self, there also seem to be no experiences — no movement, feelings, excitement, or the thousand responses of which the self is capable. From here on all experiences are of a non-relative character, meaning the experience is *it*, it is *there*, and there is nothing outside itself.

Since this is difficult to explain, I will give an example of how I came by this understanding. In the following experience, I realized the great importance of having no self and of giving no heed to even the most marvelous of events. The northeast portion of my camp sloped to a small meadow. Directly across, the meadow gave way to a steep descent that led to a lower valley. From the top of the descent a stream gushed from the side of the mountain having made its way underground from a lake a half mile away. Near the outlet of the stream, one could get a view of the valley and surrounding hills, laden with boulders, trees, and patches of wild grass. The east wall of this valley was a tall imposing mountain of solid rock that turned red in the sunset. The locals called it, Thunder Mountain.

I often went to this spot, not only to take in the view but to watch for the animals that came to drink. This day, however, I had been collecting firewood and only stopped to rest.

Since there was nothing unusual going on at the stream, I stood looking out over the valley, gazing at nothing in particular, when I noticed a peculiar gathering of intensity in the air somewhere over the valley. Whatever it was, it was gathering itself together from all parts and in doing so, was expanding outwards, obliterating everything in its path. At the same time, it grew to such a pitch of vibratory, almost electrical, intensity that it exerted a magnetic pull on my body. At first glimpse, it appeared to be the familiar Oneness, but as it grew in intensity I realized it was something else, something I did not recognize at all. The Oneness had always revealed itself through a medium, but if this was the Oneness, it now had no medium and was magnified a thousand times over, a magnification that could not be endured. But whatever its reality, I knew that to be caught in the path of its expansion was to be drawn into it like a speck of dust. I thought my time had come, and that despite the mystery of what remained, it would remain no longer. Another second and the light would go out forever — the light of the eye that beheld this wonder. Somehow I knew this should not be so, yet there was nothing that could be done. I could not look away for there was nowhere else to look; there was no energy to move; and within, all was still and motionless: no response, no thoughts, and no feelings. What would be, would be.

At the threshold of disintegration something happened. With nothing more to guide it than itself, the body turned away, made an about-face that once more confronted it with the forest and the wood to be gathered. So I went on my way, but did not get far before I had to sit down, because the body was so weak and shaken I thought it might yet fall apart.

This experience occurred a number of times while I was in the mountains and each time I could not get over the mechanism of "turning away." Though I was being pulled in the direction of this intensity, of myself I could not have pulled away or turned away. But turn I did, and always at the last moment.

I never knew how to evaluate this experience, but each time it occurred, I thought the end had come and that the light would go out forever — the light of all consciousness, original and unoriginal. It would have meant a total blackout such as I had experienced before, a blackout in which there is absolutely nothing; an annihilation more complete than just the loss of self — and what this means I have no idea.

I felt the need of great strength in order to enter the intensity without the light going out, but what kind of strength is this and how could it be acquired? Perhaps it was the strength needed to bear the vision — to enter into God — but I did not know for sure, nor could I imagine how one could see God face to face and live. To come upon such a requirement could make a man despair and turn away. Nevertheless, I felt sure that whatever had brought me this far would give me the strength to go all the way. In my journal I called this experience a "crack in the door."

Chapter 4

The snows came early that year. After two stormy days, I awoke in the night to hear a great silence — a silence only snow can bring. The storm left a foot of snow that so transformed the woods and surrounding mountains, it was like a totally new terrain, a place I had never been before. For several days the roads were snowbound, but by the time the snow had partially melted, black heavy clouds hung low above the trees, and when the Ranger's car drove up, I knew what he was going to say.

From time to time the Ranger had stopped by to swap animal stories, and each time he never failed to tell a story of someone he'd had to "dig out" because he stayed too long. Since another snowfall was imminent, it was necessary to leave before the roads iced up and I would be snowbound, for how long this time, he did not know.

So after packing my gear and stuffing the remaining nuts into the hollows and holes of my forest friends, I stood there taking a last look around, knowing the best months of my life had come to an end, an end that had been inevitable from the beginning. I knew that although I should return many times to this spot, it would never be the same. I had learned long ago that the essence of life's movement was not contentment or security; rather, it was growth, change, and challenge wherein the external circumstances of life merely reflect the needs of each moment in the thrust of life's flow. What I would find down the mountain I did not know, but I was sure nothing could ever again alter the flow I had discovered in the mountains, a flow that would continue to take me "whithersoever it goeth."

My first destination was a campground overlooking the sea. As beautiful a site as it was, I seemed unable to appreciate the surroundings because I noticed a subtle change in the object now being picked up by the 3D glasses. Instead of seeing the Oneness into which all separateness dissolved, everything now dissolved into an inexplicable emptiness. Where, for so many months there had been "something," now there was nothing.

In time, this emptiness became increasingly pronounced and difficult to live with. Without an "inner" life or the slightest movement within, the seeing had become my life; I was totally dependent upon it, and without it, I had not a thing to fall back on.

But if the constant sight of emptiness was tedious and difficult to live with, it was as nothing compared to what I came upon one morning as I walked along the beach.

Suddenly I was aware that all life around me had come to a complete standstill. Everywhere I looked, instead of life, I saw a hideous nothingness invading and strangling the life out of every object and vista in sight. It was a world being choked to death by an insidious void, whereby every remaining movement was but the final throe of death. The sudden withdrawal of life, left in its wake a scene of death, dying, and decay so monstrous and terrible to look upon, I thought to myself: no man can see this and live! My body froze to the spot.

The immediate reaction was to ward off the view, to make the vision go away by finding some explanation or meaning for it; in a word, to rationalize it away. But as I reached for each defense, the knowledge that I had not a single weapon dawned on me like a sudden blow to the head, and in the same instant I understood this thing called self: it is man's defense against seeing absolute nothingness, against seeing a world devoid of life, a life devoid of God. Without a self, man is defenseless against such a vision, a vision he cannot possibly live with.

Realizing I could no longer project a single defense, I waited for some reaction, especially an inner movement of fear. Somehow I knew that with the birth of fear, self would spring alive with all its weaponry, for it was now obvious that fear — the mother of all inventions — was the core around which the self was built and upon which its life so depended that self and fear were here, all but indistinguishable. But when no reaction came, when there was no movement of fear, I concluded the self had been frozen and entombed within me in full consciousness of its state of immobility, death, and total helplessness. Unwittingly I had been lured and entrapped in this monstrous state of no-self, an irreversible state because, once gone, the self can never return. Thus in these moments, surrounded by a terror I could not feel, and from which I could not escape, I seemed doomed to remain in the unlivable condition of having to stare out at a horrible nothingness without a single weapon of defense.

Until this moment, I had given no thought to the self, or where it had gone the year before; rather, my concern was what remained in its absence. From the time of its disappearance, I had known a great freedom — the freedom to come upon the Oneness which lies beyond the self. But right now, the silence within was not seen as freedom from the self, rather it was seen as an imprisoned self; a frozen, immovable self that was all part of the scene, part of the insidious nothingness choking the life out of everything. Even now it had frozen my body to the spot. How could I survive another moment?

It seems the one remaining resource was my two legs, two legs that could still run even though they felt frozen and immobile. I had learned before how to move without any need for personal volition — which is to act instantly, without thinking, without any need for self-consciousness. Once again it worked, and I found myself running down the beach. But as I did so, it was as if something else was running with me, urging, forcing me beyond all physical endurance to "Run! Run as you've never run before! You are running for your life!" And I believed it!

Now I wasn't even a jogger and had two miles to go, some of it up a steep cliff; but when I reached my car I seemed mindless of any exhaustion. Jumping in, I drove downtown and parked near the main intersection. I had decided to spend the rest of the day walking and being among my own kind — and it was good to be there.

Since this was a university town, the downtown section was full of young people. On the sidewalk of one corner, a jazz-band was playing with full amplifiers; further on was a more subdued trio; and further yet, a solitary fiddler was playing lively Irish tunes. The shopwindows were dressed with outlandish, unique Halloween costumes, and the cafés were crowded. The bookstores, however, were as quiet as a library and in these places I didn't spend much time, but squeezed myself into one of the noisy cafés and ordered a beer. While sitting there watching the people around me, I decided that having no-self was as bad, if not worse, than having a self; because once beyond the self, a man was just as likely to come across an unlivable nothingness as he was a marvelous, unnameable "something" — as I first seemed to do. To put aside the self is a premature laying down of our weapons before we know for sure what lies ahead. It's all an insane risk. Without a self, man is totally vulnerable to the winds of chance — bode they good or ill. Looking at the young people around me, I was glad they had a self; in fact, the greatest blessing I could wish upon all the peoples of the earth was to have a self. That way, they would never be able to see what I had just seen and what no man could see and live with.

For myself, of course, it was too late. I had survived
this time, but who knows what tomorrow may bring? Fortunately I could not think a moment ahead or imagine how
anything more could go wrong; instead, I tried to figure out
where, in the past, I had somehow made a wrong turn that
had brought me to such an impasse and landed me in this
terrible predicament. All I could think of was: that I had
trusted God too much...but is this really possible?

I used to wonder if we could ever abandon too much
of our self to God, or if there was a limit beyond which a
man should not go. Should we abandon our mind, our
memory, our whole existence — forfeit all we know in order
to come upon him, the Unknown? It is one thing to abandon our will in the form of accepting trials and tribulations,
but it is quite another to be without a will or any energy to
call our own. To give one's self to God is one thing, but to
have him accept it, is a terrible thing — or so I now understood. The whole problem is that I had given myself over to
"something" I didn't even know, and why I did not anticipate the present outcome is something else I didn't know.
Thus, there was only one way to account for this predicament: in thinking I had abandoned myself to God, I had, in
reality, abandoned myself to nothing. So, yes indeed, it is
possible to trust God too much, but only if there is no God,
only if there is nothing beyond the self.

But if there is no God, then all along I had only been
trusting myself — so which was worse? Somehow they both
had a way of leading to similar dead ends. But if you can't
trust either of these, what's left? That was the real question:
if there is no self and no God, what then? I had just seen
"what then" and couldn't live with that either. There's nothing blissful about sheer nothingness — even Sartre declared
it nauseous — so what it all boils down to is the fact that the
only thing we can trust in life is...well, money.

With a self or without a self, with a belief or without a
belief, to survive, man needs money or material goods; it's

the ultimate compensation, perhaps, for having no self and no God. We blame greed on the self, but it may not work that way at all; materialism may not stem from the self but from the nothingness that lies beyond the self. So when there is not self and no God what else can we do with our lives but make them economically feasible? And for myself, I thought the sooner I got into this financial game the better off I'd be — after all, life must go on despite our worst experiences of it.

Back at camp, however, I was not so optimistic. I had a messed-up life on my hands and coping with the here-and-now made for some very bad days. I tried to keep busy so as not to remember what had happened and, above all, I stayed away from the beaches because there was no life there anymore. What I had to deal with now was this frozen self, the very idea of which could be personified as "icy fingers" of an unknown terror and dread that had a way of appearing when my mind was unoccupied. Though seemingly held in abeyance and never approaching too close, I knew they were lurking in the background of my mind and were liable to appear at any time. Right here, I realized how totally my life depended upon the toughness of the immovable stillness within, for I knew that the slightest feeling of fear or panic and these icy fingers, which were like sudden flashes of light in my head, would invade me entire being, resulting in madness. But I had no control over this silence, it wasn't even me, rather, it was all that remained of a self-that-was. Thus, my fate now lay in the precarious balance between the stillness within and an unknowable terror that could suddenly apear in my mind.

To avoid any possible confrontation, I tried to keep very busy, and with four children this was not hard to do. More than once they had been my lifesavers, for despite all the quarreling, dirty rooms, and loud music, they always kept my feet on the ground and my nose to the grindstone. Right now, just being around them was all that mattered.

Consequently, an upcoming date to make a retreat with the Hermit Monks on the Big Sur had to be cancelled; the last thing I needed was solitude and silence. So I got on the phone and told Brother there was no possible way my car could make it up their steep hill. He laughed and said, "If you could see some of the 'things' that make it up this hill, you'd have to believe in miracles; besides, if you can't make it up, leave the car down and we'll send Brother E to pick you up." So that was that. How could I possibly tell him about these "icy fingers" following me around? For sure he would have told me to go to the hospital instead.

The day I drove down the coast, a big storm hit the Big Sur. Twice I had to pull over and wait for a lull in order to see beyond the windshield. After the second pull-over, I decided to stop at the next phone and tell them I couldn't make it; if it was this bad down the hill, imagine what it must be like going up the hill! Unfortunately, the storm suddenly abated, and by the time I arrived at the foot of the monks' grade, it had become a clear and beautiful day.

I decided to wait for Brother E who came down every day at noon to meet the mailman; I thought he could follow me up and be of help should I have any trouble. After helping him unload the pig slop — which the monks donate to their neighboring farmer — Brother got in his car and told me to follow, "In case," he said, "you have any trouble, at least I can keep going!"

At first everything went okay but when we got to the worst vertical upgrade, Brother suddenly set his brakes, got out of the car, came back and told me to do the same, because he had to put a new blade on his tractor — which was to the right of us, half over the cliff already.

Now I did not know if my handbrake would hold, in fact I was not sure how long the footbrake would hold, so I shouted at him to "Move it over because I'm going through!" But how could he move over? To the immediate left was a steep embankment, and to the right, a sheer drop;

it was obvious that somebody had to give. What happened next is called the "big squeeze," but once beyond this delay, the rest of the way up was a breeze.

Arriving on top, instead of being relieved however, I saw the whole situation as positively ludicrous; after all, my car was probably in better shape than some of the clunkers the monks were driving. Then too, the road had been newly paved. So there I stood, possibly the most reluctant retreatant ever to come up the hill, and had I known what lay ahead I would have gone back down. We never know the time or place where our destiny will catch up with us, nor could I have imagined why, for me, it would be here on the monks' hillside.

The first two or three days went by so well, I thought I had finally won out; but on the afternoon of the third or fourth day the icy fingers came back, and in a moment of bravado I decided it was time to have it out with whatever it was. I could not keep running from this thing all my life; I had to get it out in the open, face it head-on and deal with it, because I could no longer stand its continual lurking around every corner of my day. I decided to go outside, sit on the hillside and stare it in the face, until one of us gave way — or went away.

Now I cannot convey what it is like to stare at some invisible horror when you don't know what it is. Just knowing what it is may be all the defense you need; but when you've gone through your list of name-calling and it does no good, you just have to resign yourself to not knowing and face it anyway. This thing I had to stare down was simply a composite of every connotation we have of "terror," "dread," "fear," "insanity," and things of this order. In a word, it was a mental, psychological killer.

Although I knew this whole drama was only in my head, my thinking mind was all but numb in its presence; but for this reason, the thing seemed also on the outside, so I could personify it as icy fingers, which were like darting tentacles of light. Though it was unlocalized, it was easy to stare at because it was all around me, there was no place else to look.

At one point I thought it might be a raving, maniacal self wanting to get back in. At other times it seemed only to be the fear of having a stroke, or fear of insanity; again, it might only be the menopause. But I'm convinced it wouldn't have done the least good to know; by this time absolutely nothing could be done about it, for whatever its mission in my life, it was going to be accomplished right here and now.

The longer I watched these fingers the closer they approached, sometimes almost touching, then suddenly retracting; they seemed to be in constant movement (in my mind). Initially, my reaction was only the appearance of goose bumps with a shudder now and then, but later my head grew hot, so hot, in fact, it felt like it was on fire and visually, all I could see were stars. Then I felt my feet begin to freeze with the freezing sensation spreading upward to encompass all but my head. Finally I fell back against the hill in a convulsive condition with my heart beating wildly.

I knew I was going to crack, crack wide open, but never having done this before I had no idea what would happen. I lay there waiting, endlessly waiting for the crack to occur while, physically, this thing was tearing me to pieces. Within, there was not a single movement, not a fear, not a feeling of any kind. At times I tried to focus on this great stillness, but it never gave me any sense of strength or confidence; instead, it was as unconcerned as if a mere fly were buzzing overhead. It seems that my body had been left to bear the brunt of an assault which neither the mind nor the emotions could take part in. Yet, had they been there, the result might have been worse — I do not know. But so bad was my physical condition, I never doubted for a moment that only a miracle could save me; yet, I never expected one, didn't even hope for one, nor could my mind have formulated the simplest prayer. All I wanted to do was get it over with — to die if necessary.

I was not aware of the moment when the dreadful thing departed, for the next thing I was aware of was a profound stillness wherein there was no physical sensation at all. After a while, something must have turned my head. I found myself looking, eye-level, at a small, yellow wildflower, no more than twelve inches away.

I cannot describe that moment of seeing; words could never do it justice. Let us just say it smiled — like a smile of welcome from the whole universe. In the intensity of the smile, the light of the eye did not go out, nor was there a physical body to turn away; finally, the great intensity could be endured.

It took a while to realize my body was still lying on the hill because, initially, I seemed not to have one. For all I knew, I could have been a weed or a pebble on the hillside. After a time, however, the body became obvious and I decided to test it, to see if it was intended to move again. Once more it moved without thought, only this time, the return of physical sensation was accompanied by a mild shock. When I got to my feet, it was gratifying to feel the body as relaxed as if nothing had happened. Thus, I climbed the hill the same as I had gone down the hill, but only physically, for in reality, something had gone down the hill that never returned.

Apart from the absence of the dreadful thing which I never saw again, I came up the hill without any sense of true existence. Though I searched everywhere in what should have been my being, I now felt there was nothing substantial there, nothing left that I had not experienced as either dissolving, or suddenly disappearing and leaving nothing in its place. As for "that" which remained, I had no idea what it was, where it was, or even, if it was. Though something obviously climbed the hill, it would be a long time before I discovered its true nature; for the moment, all I knew was that a great change had taken place.

In retrospect, I came to regard this event on the hillside as an initiation into what I have called The Great Passageway, an unusual state of existence to be described in the next chapter.

A few days after this event, I found myself complaining to Father L that I couldn't keep hold on my existence anymore. So he asked me, "Well, what about your empirical existence — your empirical self — is it sitting here talking to me or not?" I told him, "Visually it would appear to be so, but if I close my eyes, I can't see it anymore." Then I told him of how, during prayer or any time I was inactive, my body would melt away, or seem to dissolve, so that if I did not keep my eyes on it, I wouldn't know I had one. With that, he threw up his arms and said, "Oh, God, that's far out!" But while I went on complaining, he sat there musing to himself about what would happen to scholastic theology if science proved there was no such thing as a permanent substance in matter!

Finally I found myself trying to reassure him. I suggested that man's notion of matter-versus-spirit might turn out to be the reverse of what it has traditionally been thought to be; namely, God might turn out to be pure matter (or permanent substance) and matter might turn out to be pure spirit (or God); in other words, matter and spirit may actually be identical. What this would mean is that the scientist turns out to be the contemplative, or deep-sea fish, swimming around looking for the Sea he is already in; while the contemplative turns out to be the unwitting scientist who has already come upon permanent substance without realizing it.

But Father wasn't listening; he was off on one of his theological head-trips and I knew where it would end. He would eventually draw a blank and then just sit there and stare out the window, over the hillside and out to the sea, into which every theory and insight has a way of eventually dissolving and disappearing. So I left him to discover his own dead ends, and went on my way to figure out how one's body could be visibly apparent as long as the eyes were open, but in no way apparent when the eyes were closed.

Perhaps I should add that the continual melting away of the body was very different from the out-of-the-body experiences I had heard of. Apparently these latter experiences reveal a division between the higher and lower self, whereas in my experience, there was no such division — obviously there was no self left to be divided. Because of these experiences, however, I eventually came to look upon the body — as well as all visible form — as somewhat ethereal or illusive in nature; and because form itself is composed of an unknowable, untouchable substance that remains permanent throughout all change, it seemed to me it was this substance that remained in the absence of self. At any rate, the whole empirical argument for self-existence melted away once and for all on the hillside, and to this day remains irretrievable.

Before venturing further, I must mention that there was a certain irony in the above event taking place on the monks' hillside. Some two years before, when the monks first opened their retreat house to women, it was first necessary to gain permission from the prior of the monastery — to be screened, in other words. To do this, I made a special trip down the coast for my first meeting with Father Prior who, after graciously giving his permission, asked me, "Well, what do you hope to gain by making a retreat with us?" I told him I didn't know for sure, but for the last year I had felt, interiorly, as if I were getting ready for a great explosion. . .suddenly he stiffened in his chair, "Oh, for God's sake don't do it here!" he said, "We're just trying to get the monks used to having women around and that would ruin it, literally 'blow it' for everyone."

Now I had no idea what Father Prior thought I meant by a "great explosion," but knowing he had been a doctor of chemistry before becoming a monk, I thought he must have had some bad experiences that might have colored any other connotation of the term. For me, the great explosion was supposed to have been a marvelous spiritual blossoming — and preferably one with creative overtones. Never in my wildest dreams did I suspect it was my 'self' about to be blasted into a million irretrievable pieces. Such an expectation was not on my Christian agenda, and to do it on the monks' hillside? Certainly it would have been a disgrace to the whole Church. But as I have said, one never knows the time or place when destiny will catch up; that I should meet mine on the monks' mountain was certainly an ironical event, one I could not have foreseen, but one that was not lost on me.

Chapter 5

Although the mechanisms of change that occurred during the journey are unknown to me, I was immediately able to recognize either the presence of something new or the absence of something old; and the change that took place on the hillside — which began the second half of this journey — can best be understood in relation to the changes that occurred at the beginning.

Initially, with the falling away of all sense of having an interior life, there had been a turning outward to the seeing of Oneness and the falling away of everything particular and individual. The seeing itself was not located within, but first seemed to be like 3D glasses imposed upon my ordinary vision, and later, localized as a seeing "on top of the head." Acclimating to this new outward way of life lasted almost a year, before a second major change occurred on the monks' hillside. The essence of this second change was a doing away with everything on the outside, which meant a disappearance of the great Oneness I had seen, as well as the 3D glasses that could now no longer focus on a single object or idea. Thus, the seeing, no longer localized, was like a faculty suddenly struck blind. Altogether this adds up to living in a state wherein there is nothing on the inside and nothing on the outside; it's a state of total unknowing and a very difficult state to live in and cope with; however, I shall try to describe it.

Initially, the experience of finding emptiness every-where I looked had been merely bewildering because it was relatively new. No doubt, the reason my mind could no longer focus on particular objects or ideas was due to the total emptiness I found there — an emptiness that no longer gave way or dissolved into Oneness. But as the days and weeks went by, without any let-up or compensation, this state of affairs became increasingly difficult to live with, for the continual seeing of sheer nothingness within and with-out made for an unspeakable sterility, an unendurable mode of existence.

After a time I felt as if my head (my mind, my brain) had been placed in a vise so I could no longer move it at all. I could not look backward to the past, or from side to side in my desperate attempts to focus on something in the im-mediate present. All I could do was look straight ahead; but straight ahead there was nothing to see, for I felt I had been blindfolded, so that before me was only a dark, empty void.

Because my mind could focus on nothing, nor hang on to anything knowable, it soon felt as if my brain was on fire or that some terrible pressure behind the eyes was forcing me to go blind; and this relentless pressure in my head was like a terrible taskmaster constantly commanding me to "See! You MUST see! You CAN see! Look and see!" It pounded away day after day, week after week, month after month until I knew I would never be released from this hor-rible condition, nor escape the terrible taskmaster unless I did, eventually, "see." But see what? What was I supposed to be looking for? And how could I ever see when I no longer had eyes to see? Constantly before me there was only emptiness and nothingness.

Because of its terrible restrictiveness, I called this state of affairs, The Great Passageway. I had no idea where I was or where I was going. If the first part of the journey was, in fact, the movement from self to no-self, this second half was the movement from no-self to nowhere, for I do not believe self enters the Passageway because it could not endure what must here be endured.

Instinctively I knew this was a very dangerous condition, for I felt I was treading on the brink of insanity, or some narrow precipice between life and death, and that survival was totally dependent upon no-self — that tough, immovable stillness of everything within. Somehow I knew that the slightest movement within might suddenly throw me off balance and I would slip away forever.

At times it was tempting to regard this great stillness as God, but I think I was mistaken and later shall explain why. Another temptation was to regard the terrible taskmaster as possibly God, for despite its relentless, merciless, non-compensatory commands to "see — and KEEP GOING," I instinctively felt it knew where it was going and what it was doing. There were moments when I thought of going in search of some type of medication to relieve my burning brain, but since I had never taken drugs in my life, I had no idea of what they might do; furthermore, I knew that drugs themselves know not what they do, nor could I believe any doctor knew any more than his drugs. So I trusted the taskmaster to bring me through, in order for the journey to take its own course and end in its own time; otherwise, to abort it for any reason might mean never completing the Passage and never knowing what, if anything, lay on the other side.

Another reason I discounted the use of drugs was that I felt the greatest need to stay constantly awake and alert at a time when my personal energies were at the lowest possible ebb. On one such occasion I merely watched — as an unmoved observer watches a light grow distant and fade away altogether — the choiceless ebbing away of the last ounce of physical energy I owned. It was then I learned that the passing away, and becoming, of anything is not the way life really works; for despite the coming and going of what we call life and energy, something remains that never moves nor participates in these passages. Something that is just there, just watching, and "that" which remains, is true life, while all the energies that come and go are not true life. But what is "that" that remains and observes? And what is it that endures this passage? What is this form that keeps melting away? And what is it that remains when there is no self? Certainly it was not me — I had been the one to pass away. Could it be God then? Well, if it was, I did not know for I could not see a single thing.

This observing of my own coming and going taught me an important lesson. It taught me the meaning of the taskmaster's urgent insistence to "Keep going! Move straight ahead! Don't stop for anything!" which I never understood until this occasion. In watching the final ebbing away of life, I felt absolutely no concern. Nothing in me responded to this observation until it finally occurred to me that at some point I might be going, and never again be coming. But such a prospect can hardly be frightening to a dead man; I had not sufficient energy to care. My life was now in the hands of some mysterious fate and there was no choice but to let the chips fall where they may. But even in such a choiceless moment as death, I knew I had not yet seen, and that there was no way I would be allowed to slip away forever until the journey had been completed. Thus, I realized I would somehow have to keep going, keep dragging my feet around, for even if I couldn't see how this passage could possibly be completed in the here-and-now, the prospect of spending a sightless eternity was equally unappealing.

But how to keep going was one of the most difficult and trying aspects of the Passageway; it was a time of learning how to survive without having the slightest sense of personal energy.

To begin with, I found it necessary to keep constantly occupied with resources outside my own mind, for in this Passageway I could not truly think, reflect, or formulate a single idea or thought; yet I suddenly discovered I could listen to the thoughts and ideas of others while maintaining a perfectly silent and unthinking mind, for my understanding of practical affairs was unimpaired. As long as I listened, my mind was silent and there was no pressure on it to "be silent." From here, I next discovered I could also read books that demanded no thinking and left my mind without pressure. Though I couldn't handle philosophy, I found it helpful as well as interesting to read every book on mountain climbing the library had to offer.

Finally, the day came when I discovered I could also talk and converse with this same silent, unthinking mind, but only as long as it came right "off the top" — that is, spontaneously, without thinking or reflecting. At first, such conversations were necessarily brief and limited to practical affairs, but in time, the knack of talking off the top of the head became a permanent function. Later I called it my "non-reflective mind" and gradually recognized it as far superior to the ordinary thinking mind, for it allows a great clarity which I shall try to describe further on.

Right now, however, I was just beginning to discover listening and reading as a way to ward off the pressure in my brain. In a word I was slowly learning how to cope with life in the Passageway so as to keep going and thus avoid the danger of inactivity, passivity, and non-doing.

It was due to these dangers that I eventually came upon a new type of activity, the activity of an unthinking, unknowing mind in which there are no self-invested energies, no goal but survival, and not an ounce of satisfaction anywhere. It was right here — unknown to me at the time — that I was beginning to emerge into a whole new way of life, which no intellect can fashion or even imagine possible until it comes upon this life from the other side of knowing — which is from the side of unknowing.

The worst part of the Passageway, by far, was its non-compensatory aspect. (There was, as well, its four-month duration. A few days or week, okay, but almost four full months of being in a mental straitjacket verged, day after day, on the brink of the intolerable.) Years before, I had come upon a passage in a book describing a state-of-unknowing in which the author defined it as "complete psychological dissociation without compensation" or some such phrase as that. At the time, I could not imagine what he was talking about, but felt sure it was something terrible, and was glad I have never known any condition as dire as this sounded. But here, during the Passage, I recalled the statement because it seemed to epitomize my present situation better than any words my mind could formulate. Though I do not know its psychological usage — the author was a psychologist — I took it for my own condition of being completely cut off (dissociated) from the known, the self, without any compensating factor to take the place of the emptiness so encountered. It meant a state of no feelings, no energies, no movements, no insights, no seeing, no relationships with anything — nothing but absolute emptiness everywhere you turn. The utter sterility of this state is all but humanly unendurable, especially for any length of time, and to bear the burden of complete unknowing is a weight that moment by moment threatened to crush me, although crush me without bringing death. I had already seen that death was no release because sooner or later the Passageway must be completed, and I would never be free of the burden-of-unknowing until I could see.

This state cannot be compared to a Dark Night for it is more (and far worse) than the purification of the mind and will in its ignorance of the Unknown; rather, it is a radical psychological state wherein the mind cannot even dwell on the known, much less the Unknown. Although empirical reality remained, it could not be focused on perceptually, nor could individual objects be focused on visually. Instead, the usual objects of the mind were seen in a global sense, which made for some tense moments, particularly when driving or when shopping in a market. Such a state might be akin to the infant's outlook on the world wherein he visually sees what the adult sees, but lacks the adult's perception and focusing ability because his mind is still in the non-relative state of unknowing. But for a mature, relative, knowing mind to return to this non-relative condition, while maintaining itself within the range of normalcy, is a feat of gigantic proportions. Yet, oddly enough, the saving grace — at least grace that is knowable and obvious — is the conditioned mind itself.

I had always been antipathetic toward the behaviorists' conditioned model of human thought and behavior, but in the Passageway I understood its importance as the very condition of sanity, and that the preconditioned habits of a balanced, integrated, adult mind were absolutely essential for making the passage. Hence, the years prior to taking the journey — years of trying and testing the psychic balance — were of the utmost importance; so much so that everything now depended upon this stability of conditioned behavior. With only two or three exceptions, I experienced nothing that could be called a divine, strengthening grace. For the most part, I walked under the weighty, enormous burden of such total unknowing that just the ability to keep going was beyond comprehension itself.

On the few occasions I came upon divine relief, there was no mistaking its origin. These events occurred toward the end of the Passageway — a fact I can only see in retrospect — and were always preceded by a piling up of all the intolerable aspects of this state: its duration, its apparent endlessness, the fatigue, the pressure behind the eyes, the precarious state of sanity, the total lack of understanding; in a word, the terrible burden of unknowing and unseeing. All this and more suddenly became overwhelming, and under its monstrous weight, something collapsed. Whatever remains without a self, disintegrated, melted away like the thinnest veil to the infinite. It was the obliteration of all but the joyous, humorous smile of the divine, a smile that somehow was completely subjective. The most poignant, immediate word of description was "melting" — a veritable melting, in which God was all that remained.

Despite this momentary reprieve, I would soon return to the usual condition and therefore had to discount this as the final seeing. The melting away of what remained was evidently not the seeing that had been demanded. If anything, it struck me as a merciful scolding from the taskmaster, as if my own hardness had melted and it was saying, "I told you, you could see! You are seeing all the time — and you know this! You cannot possibly doubt it." Indeed, there was no doubt. The nature of the passage does not permit of intellectual doubt; but then, neither does it permit of certitude. In truth, it permits of nothing.

Apart from these two reprieves, the mind was immersed in a dire void wherein it had nowhere to look since it could focus on nothing. Here I was reminded of Christ's saying he had nowhere to lay his head; meaning (to me at least) there was nothing in this world on which he could truly focus his attention, nothing to which his mind could be either perceptually or conceptually attached.

Eventually it became clear that this Passageway was beyond despair, and even beyond insanity; for "who" is left to go insane or "what" remains to experience despair? If self had been alive, it would have gone mad on the spot; and if nothing else, I would have jumped at any chance to throw in the towel and back out. But our psychological notions of despair and anxiety are mere toys of self-defense compared to the burden-of-unknowing, against which there isn't a single defense; nor is there, for that matter, anything or anyone left to defend. To have had a self would have been most compensating, for self *is* man's compensation for a state of unknowing — or so I was now convinced.

Nevertheless, the true mechanism of surviving the Passageway is not known to me. Self was dead, immovably silent. The taskmaster (merely a pressure on my brain) kept demanding that my mind be still and "See!" And my body was ingesting health foods in its feeble attempt to compensate for the loss of self-energy. Probably the mechanism of getting through is built into the Passageway itself, if for no other reason than that it's the only way to go. There are no options and no outs, no death and no insanity; it's there and you're part of it, and that's what is — just a Passageway.

By the end of four months I had learned, to some extent, how to cope with this state of affairs. By "cope" I do not mean an act of resignation, but merely an acclimation to the inevitable. For all I knew, I might have to live this way the rest of my life, so I did my best to work up some commensurate routine in order to keep going. Most important, perhaps, is the fact that I eventually became acclimated to the emptiness when I discovered that time alone took care of it, for after a while it was hardly noticed anymore.

It seems that when the emptiness of existence is no longer important, "doing" becomes everything. Thus, during the Passageway the emphasis shifted from simple existence — such as I had known it in the mountains — to doing, which now became a way of life. Nevertheless, during this time, while walking through the hills, I sometimes came upon a certain sadness concerning the rock-bottom emptiness of man and nature. I felt bad about the fact that man lives his whole life in the false expectation that some ultimate reality lies hidden somewhere behind, beneath, or beyond what is. And I remembered my own life of searching and looking and now saw what a complete waste it had been.

All the experiences of my life had been nothing more than a head-trip, a great psychological hoax, a pointless circular affair whereby I was now back where I started — not knowing any more about life or God than the day I was born. To think of all the wasted energy: studying, speculating, practicing, looking, striving, suffering, experiencing, and all of it? A perfect waste! In truth, everything man knows is one hundred percent speculation and wishful thinking, egged blindly on, no doubt, by a self persistently demanding its own survival. What a trick of the mind! What total deception! And what man born has not been led by the nose and fallen into this trap — a trap which *is* the self? And yet, what lies beyond the self? If emptiness and nothingness is the whole truth and nothing but the truth, then man is entitled to his self and his deceptions; he must have this compensation for an ultimate reality that turns out to be sheer nothingness.

Again and again in these walks through the hills and along the river, I wondered too if there was any last vestige in me called "trust in God." Initially I had been willing to give up this thing called self because I was somehow assured that God lay beyond it. So I had trusted and I had loved and, until the Great Passageway, had not been deceived. But now that trust had finally been broken to pieces for I could find it nowhere. In its place was a gentle disappointment and the final acceptance of what is — which means: what you see is all you get.

It also means just the simple doing of whatever lies before you to do at each moment of the day, with no looking around, searching underneath, or probing behind. Just the doing of what is immediately under your nose to do, and not a thing more.

So this was the end of the line. I had finally come upon the great truth: that all was empty; that self had merely filled in the emptiness; and that all man's words were empty labels foraged by a mind that doesn't know a thing about its world and cannot tolerate a state of unknowing. Well, I could live with this. Although coming upon these great truths had almost cost me my life, finally I was discovering how to live with them; after all, this is what the journey was all about: to find the truth and nothing less. I might continue to be sorry for all those still wasting their lives in the unwitting search for emptiness, yet I felt no zeal to inform them of the truth ahead of time; knowing the truth doesn't necessarily make for a better life, a life that must go on whether there's any truth in it or not. Thus, with this "see-ing" I felt sure I had come full circle and could finally put this whole business aside and go out and make some money.

Chapter 6

It was late winter and the muddy waters of the river were jammed with burnt debris from a mountain fire two years before. Every day, my son and I would stand on the banks to measure the height of the swelling waters, and then he would use the swift moving logs as targets for his rocks, for he had a strong pitch and a good eye. One day, however, he was late in coming, so I walked down and sat on the river's edge, watching the dead wood in its speedy descent to the sea. With neither reason nor provocation, a smile emerged on my face, and in the split second of recognition I "saw" — finally I saw, and knew I had seen. I knew: *the smile itself, that which smiled, and that at which it smiled, were One* — as indistinguishably one as a trinity without division. And what I saw was merely how this was so. There was no insight, no vision, no movement of anything, but a seeing that was as natural and spontaneous as a smile on a face — not another thing more. In my journal I called this "the grin-of-recognition."

Since what I had seen could not be retained, grasped, or held onto by the mind, I continued to watch the river as it cleaned out the mountain debris and washed down the banks in its determined flow to meet with the sea. Later I took a walk and saw that, although the Great Passageway was now over, everything looked as usual. Nothing had changed and it was good to see this was so. If there was anything marvelous or spectacular about this seeing, it was the fact that everything was as usual and that nothing had changed. It meant that I too was as usual, and had arrived at the end of the passage, normal, whole, and sane. I was grateful for this; it was almost too good to be true. And yet, how could it be otherwise when "that" which remains at the end of the passage is Itself normal, whole, and sane!

It may seem strange to have rejoiced more in the ending of the passage than in what had been revealed there. It must be understood, however, that I could not rejoice in what had been revealed because I could not grasp it, hang on to it. It was so utterly simple, so completely obvious, and so totally subjective, it was impossible to understand why I had not seen it before, and yet, there is no way I could come to this seeing of my own accord. It had to be revealed.

What I learned was that the unknown object (of the smile) was identical with the subject, and not only that, but the smile itself was identical with these. And what is the smile? It is that which remains when there is no self. The smile is neither the unknown subject or object, yet it is identical with it. It is that aspect of the Unknown which is manifest. The implications of this seeing are tremendous and yet, they cannot be grasped by the mind.

Thus, the full implication of this seeing was not immediately apparent. Though the pressure behind the eyes never returned and my mind knew an effortless silence, life went on as usual; I was not aware of any real change. Then, about a week or so later while on my way to catch an early morning bus, the usual emptiness was replaced by something else, something that was not localized as a presence, but something more pervasive and intense than even the Oneness I had seen with the 3D glasses. Immediately I took this for an absolute sham, a trap, a trick of the mind; besides, it came too late, I was now beyond all such enticements that had landed me nothing but trouble in the past. So I ignored it, refused to give it space or look at it; and if

I'd had a self, I probably would have felt toward it a feeling of disdain. I walked on, looking straight ahead, and went to work.

But "it" also went to work, and so surrounded me I could hardly divert my eyes from it. This went on for several days until I knew that the greater my attempts to ignore it, the greater it increased the pressure to "Look!" So eventually I did look, and the moment I did so, it vanished and was gone, but in the same instant I knew why.

You cannot look at what Is, for it cannot become an object to the mind, nor for that matter, can it be a subject. What Is is "that" which can never be a subject or an object. Thus, the moment you look with your relative (subject-object-oriented) mind, what Is is gone because you have tried to make it an object, and it won't work. The relative mind cannot apprehend this reality; only a non-relative mind sees because what Is is equally non-reflective or non-self-conscious. Since what Is is all that Is, it has nothing to see outside itself nor within itself and thus, has no such thing as a relative, reflective, self-conscious mind. Nor is it a mind at all, nor consciousness, for no man knows *what* it is, only *that* it Is. Therefore, once we have been rid of a reflective, relative, self-conscious mind, then and only then can we come upon what Is: *that which sees and is seen and the act of seeing itself are ONE.*

It seems the pressure to "look" was a pressure on the relative mind that was seemingly put out of commission during the Passageway, when it was unable to focus on or retain a single object in mind. Thus, when finally and suddenly confronted with something to look at, there was a mental reluctance to do so. It were as if I had been asked to regress or look backward, and I was extremely wary of doing so; after all, I didn't want to go on any more journeys if I didn't have to. Nevertheless, my eventual looking served a great purpose and brought about the change which the initial seeing by the river could not do.

Once I realized that what Is cannot be seen by a relative mind or become an object to itself, I had the marvelous and unique key to seeing it all the time — which was by not looking at all. It was as if the moment of its vanishing was also the final and complete close-down of the relative mind, which then heralded a new way of seeing, knowing, and acting, because now I had the key! Now I could understand, and because of this, now I could rejoice. It seems that as long as the mind is viable, it needs to enter into some form of understanding, otherwise the greatest revelation, while it would not go unnoticed, could not enter into the fullness of its human manifestation. After all the months of dire unknowing, just to know something — however incomplete — was a revelation in itself.

Part of what I understood is how what Is never comes and goes; instead, what comes and goes is the relative type of mind that is intimately entwined with the self, revolving around the self, and of its own accord can never get out of itself. But once the self has disappeared, this reflective, self-conscious mind goes with it, and what remains is what Is. You can no longer look out and see relationships, nor do you see emptiness anymore. All you see is what Is, which can at times be extremely intense, even though it is not something ecstatic, ineffable, or transcendent. On the contrary, it is obvious, natural, and somewhat ordinary for it's what we see everywhere we look. And yet, how difficult it is to see how this is so! However, though it *is* everything, there is one thing it is not: the self that blocks the view that otherwise allows us to see that which remains when self is gone — namely, what Is.

This then, is what I discovered at the end of the Passageway, and once I began to see, another new way of life opened up. There were more months of acclimating, during which I came upon many discoveries, the nature of which is difficult to communicate even though I must try.

The key discovery is what I call "doing," which is a

non-reflective, effortless activity that must be distinguished
from a deliberate, self-aware type of activity that needs constant effort and maintenance. For this reason, doing is nothing we can bring about by our own efforts and energies because doing is what follows automatically when all personal
efforts and energies have ceased. The term "effortless" here
refers to the fact that no self-energies are involved even
though, physically, we may still work up a sweat.

Learning to distinguish doing from past methods of activity is much like the conditioning process every child is
taught by its parents. In this case, self-invested activity results in emptiness because there is nothing there; whereas,
with activity in which there is no self-investment or self-
awareness, *something* is there; this activity is not empty and
is what I call, doing. The reason for using this term is because the doer, as well as that which the doer acts upon,
falls into the realm of the unknown; only the act of doing
falls into the realm of the known. We do not know "that"
which smiled or at "what" it smiled; all we know is the smile
itself — even though all three are identical. This means that
what Is can only be known because it is identical with its
acts (or doing).

Initially, the process of learning the difference between
doing and self-activity may be compared to balancing on a
walking beam, where doing means having your foot squarely
on target so there is something underfoot. Non-doing or
self-invested activity means finding no foothold, so that underfoot there is nothing. At first, making your way along
this beam is by trial and error, but eventually, walking the
beam becomes second nature; or rather you discover in
time, walking this beam is your real nature and the way you
must walk for the rest of your life. In this way then, when
there is something there (underfoot, so to speak) you know
you are on beam and are living and doing as you are supposed to be doing; but when there is nothing there, with only
a void underfoot, then you are not on beam and there is no

real doing. Thus, doing is a manifestation of something, or what Is, and non-doing (self-invested activity) is the manifestation of absolutely nothing. Where once on this journey the emphasis had been on a selfless existence, this existence was gradually seen to be empty and void and no longer of any use. But when this selfless existence disappears completely, what remains is doing, which is like a beam, a guide, and is the something that is what Is.

The content of doing, or what we do, is mapped out by the unknowable direction of the beam, which is narrow and straight and does not go in any willy-nilly direction. When on beam, we are no longer free to come and go because only self enjoys such freedoms. A choiceless state knows nothing of those usual referents of freedom. Here, there is only freedom from the self which turns out to be no freedom at all. Who is there to be free? Who is there to choose and experience, to set the goals and chart the path? The free one is now gone, and that which remains now walks the beam like an unthinking tree must grow and function in a direction already set by its nature, a nature so intelligent that it is forever completely unknowable to the human mind. Thus, knowing what to do or where to put your foot is fairly black and white: what is to be known is simply there, and what is not known is not there. In other words, what to do is built into the beam itself, so that doing is identical with its content or what it does. Thus, knowing, seeing, doing, are but a single act without a gap between.

What once created the division between doing and its content was the self with all its choices, values, judgments, ideas, and all the rest, which never gets on the beam and can't find it because it is blocked by all its so-called freedoms. Not knowing what to do, what to think, what to say, how to live is, by contrast, a state of perpetual confusion. But on this beam, what Is moves in one sure, irrevocable, and unknowable direction, so that knowing and doing are the same. Nevertheless, this way of knowing is most unusual because it is not derived from a thinking, speculating, reflecting mind; rather, whatever is before you is something either known or unknown, and in this way many things are now seen as obvious and clear which before could not have been known or seen at all. How this works is unknown to me, but that it works at all, is a source of amazement, and all part of the clarity of mind now possible when on the beam — which means being totally at one with what Is.

A second discovery, also occurring in the last months of the journey, was coming upon the silent mind. Though I was acquainted with many types of silence, and thought many times to have come upon a silent mind, this final silence was most unique and different than anything encountered before. Since I would like to try and describe it later at length — because it is so difficult to convey — I will only say for now, the silent mind seems to be a mind that no longer has a self-reflecting type of consciousness, even though all other functions of the mind remain as usual. The reason self cannot come upon this silence by its own efforts is because this silence is what remains when all self-reflection or self-awareness comes to an end. This is why I had no knowledge of this type of silence prior to taking the journey, and only recognized it for what it was, at the very end. What I also discovered at the end, was how doing actually takes the place of thinking, and thus leaves the ordinary mind silent.

Since it is difficult to do justice to the many discoveries made possible by this journey, I will only touch upon those which were most surprising and, initially, a bit disconcerting.

One such discovery was the falling away of the aesthetic sense, or that particular sense of order, beauty, and harmony we find in our surroundings and environment. As a lover of classical music — who thought music might endure beyond the spheres — I was surprised to find that silence, as well as the simple sounds of nature, surpassed the greatest works of the masters. Though I have no way to account for it, music became noise, and silence became harmony.

I also noticed that when it became impossible to focus on the singularity or discreteness of objects, all sense of their ordered arrangement disappeared. Instead, the contents of the known, with its apparent laws and rules or order, were now seen as a continuous whole, a spontaneous thrust of life which, like a single sustained note, could easily disintegrate if this tension were released. Nothing then, is predictable. That which is manifest is not subject to any rule or law outside itself — however ingenuous and obvious is its visible design.

Of its own accord, this way of seeing resulted in a simplified style of life. When there is no beauty, then no object can be valued more than another and thus, every non-utilitarian possession becomes excess baggage. The barest cell and the simple life in the woods now struck me as the only authentic way of life, and if it hadn't been for the children, I would have thrown everything to the wind and gone off. Such an ascetic ending may seem harsh, but in reality, when nothing in particular is beautiful, then everything is beautiful, a beauty we need not possess because we are already part of it, already possessed by it. Indeed, the great beauty of what Is, is its Oneness. Here, Oneness overshadows the particularity of form, making it possible to see beyond the apparent to the thing in Itself.

Another discovery occurred when I realized the necessity of taking on some semblance of self-consciousness. This dawned on me when, after spending a day in public and away from home, I saw I had forgotten to comb my hair in the morning — and it looked like hell. Thereupon I began a concerted program to try and remember myself — to remember anything in fact. By the end of the Passageway I was certain my memory had been impaired for life. It was not a failure in recall however, but seemed more like time-lapses, as if whole chunks of time were missing from the ordinary flow of life. Though I tried to find some compensatory measures to insure myself against these lapses, nothing worked. In the long run, time took care of itself because the practical memory gradually returned, and I was relieved of the impossible effort to remember myself.

Apparently, with the falling away of self-consciousness there is also a certain loss of body-awareness. This may account for the continual melting away of physical form I experienced during the latter half of the journey. In time, I acclimated to getting around this way, without a certain awareness of form. To some extent, this means taking better care of the body than ever before because now, the body tells me nothing. Though physical pain remains, I no longer have the feeling of being tired, rested, satisfied, contented, or any of the rest; somehow these familiar feelings must have subtle connections with self-consciousness. And because of this, caring for the body becomes little different than caring for a plant: when you know it needs water, food, or sunshine, you give it what it needs. You cannot "feel" for the plant, but if you are observant and know something of its mechanism, there is no problem maintaining a bodily form that is in a constant process of change and subject to the limits of time. Though I regard the body as absolutely real, I find all forms that compose the universe extremely fragile or tenuous at best, because they can so easily dissolve into the one Existent, apart from which, no form has any individual existence of its own.

Earlier I said that I often wondered if the indomitable stillness within might not be God. Somehow I seemed to hold to the notion that some day the silence of no-self would give way and reveal itself as the great Unknown — the Divine, whose inflow I had sorely missed in the absence of self. But with the eventual loss of all awareness of any stillness within, I discounted this notion because even the silence (no-self) no longer seemed to exist. However, once the journey was over, or when I realized that God does not experience himself as anything comparable to the relative experiences of the self, I saw how it could, indeed, have been God all along. It seems I had first to recognize this same stillness and emptiness as pervading everything, not just myself, before I saw its connecting link between all that Is. Thus, only when I saw how it could never be localized anywhere in particular, I finally saw how this great silence was everything and everywhere and is, truly, what Is.

In many ways this journey is comparable to a tree that has suddenly been felled, but is not yet dead; the sap (the self) still runs in its veins and only gradually, slowly, comes to a complete halt. At first, the tree merely experiences the ebbing and dwindling of its own life-giving energies, and is continually astonished to realize that while it is being emptied, it somehow continues to remain. In this way, it discovers what it once thought necessary for life — the sap — is actually not necessary at all, because even when the sap is totally gone, it does not die. But the process of dying to its ordinary way of life lends an uneasiness to the journey, for the tree never knows when, or if, it is dead, because it never experiences the in-flow of new life as the old life flows out. For me, this was the most bewildering aspect of the journey. I had fully expected that as the self disappeared and was emptied, some form of divine life would appear and fill in the emptiness. When this didn't happen, I knew I was lost.

In retrospect I now realize the full meaning of John of the Cross' continual statements to his students: that God can never truly be experienced by the faculties of man. Therefore, what we experience of God is frankly ourselves — because it's our only medium of doing so. The mind, the emotions or feelings, in a word, all our experiences in the interior life are merely our own reactions to "that" which we cannot otherwise know, see, or experience. How often then, have we mistaken ourselves for God? Or possibly, mistaken God for ourselves? There's only one way to find out, and that is to have no self at all. Since the self cannot experience God as he truly Is, then the only way to do so is to be prepared to relinquish every last thing we know of as self.

This explains why there is no experience of any divine inflow or Godlike substitute for a self-that-was, for such is not the experience of God himself, who is not self-conscious and does not experience any divine inflow. Perhaps this is why we sometimes refer to God as the great emptiness and nothingness, but God is not that, not at all. What we call emptiness and nothingness is merely a relative notion or experience, like moving from the positive to the negative before both eventually fall away and all the remains is what Is.

Nevertheless, if there is any aspect of this journey I would stress or emphasize, it is the evident necessity of finally coming to terms with the nothingness and emptiness of existence which, for me, seemed to be the equivalent of living out my life without God — or any such substitute. Only when this came about, only when the acclimation to a life without an ultimate reality was complete; when there was no hope, no trust remaining; only when I have finally to accept what is, did I suddenly realize that what is, is truth itself and all that Is. I had to discover it was only when every single, subtle, experience and idea — conscious and unconscious — has come to an end, a complete end, that it is possible for the Truth to reveal itself.

Although it was impossible to pinpoint the time or moment when the journey was over, I tend to gauge the ending when I could no longer find any relative difference between having a self and having no-self; or, the time at which all awareness of the stillness within became lost to me. Originally the awareness of no-self was merely the awareness of the absence of self with all its habitual reactions, feelings, movements, thoughts and experiences. For this reason, the awareness of no-self is purely relative to what was — the self. But as the distance between the two increases with the acclimating, accommodating process of settling down to a new way of life, the old life-with-self grows dim and fades out altogether; and with it, the relative contrast also disappears. This means there is no more awareness of the silent, still, immovable no-self that was so necessary for making the journey — especially in the Great Passageway. Thus, with the fading away of no-self I knew the journey was over; it was now but a past event, and like all the past events, it grows colorless and lifeless as it recedes from memory and loses its relevance for the here-and-now.

Compendium of the Journey

I

The moment was unheralded, unrecognized, and unknown; it was the moment "I" entered a great silence and
never returned. Beyond the threshold of the known, the
door upon self was closed, but the door upon the Unknown was opened in a fixed gaze that could not look
away. Impossible to see the self, to remember the self, or
to be self-conscious, the mind was restricted to the present moment. The more it tried to reflect back on itself,
the more overpowering the silence.

II

By steadily gazing outward upon the Unknown, the
silence abated and the emptiness of self became a joy. But
the search for the still-point — God within — revealed
not one emptiness, but two, for when there is no self,
there is no Other; without a personal self there is no personal God — without a subject, there is no object. The
still-point had vanished, and with its disappearance it
took every sense of life the self possessed — a self which
could no longer be felt to exist. What remained was not
known. There was no life, no will, no energy, no feelings,
no experiences, no within, no spiritual or psychic life.
Yet, life was somewhere because all was as usual.

III

Though it could not be localized or found within any object of sight or mind, somewhere out-of-doors, life was
flowing peacefully, assuredly. On a bluff above the sea, it
revealed itself: life is not *in* anything; rather, all things are
in life. The many are immersed in the One, even that
which remains when there is no self, this too, is absorbed
in the One. No longer a distance between self and the
other, all is now known in the immediacy of this identity.
Particulars dissolve into the One; individual objects give
way to reveal that which is the same throughout all variety
and multiplicity. To see this new dimension of life is the
gift of amazing glasses through which God may be seen
everywhere. Truly, God is all that exists — all, of course,
but the self.

IV

But what sees this Oneness and knows that it sees? The
eye that looks is not within, it is not of mind or body, it
is not of the self. Unknown and outside — at first like
glasses, then later, above the head — the eye was known
to exist, but it could neither be seen nor looked at. It did
not dissolve into Oneness — the seer and seen were not
identical. But a greater mystery still: what remained in the
absence of self? What is this that walks, thinks, and
talks? What is this that is aware of the eye upon Oneness? Among them — no-self, the eye, the Oneness — no
identity could be found.

V

At one time, the Oneness grew to an overpowering intensity, as if drawing itself together from all parts, drawing
inward and obliterating all that existed, including the eye
that saw it and that which remained. At the threshold of
extinction, the eye flickered and grew dim; instantly, that
which remained, turned away. To bear the vision, to
enter in, the light of the eye must not go out. Somehow it
must become stronger, but what kind of strength is this
and how could it be acquired? There was something still
to be done, but what? No-self is helpless; it has no
strength; it is not the light of the eye nor the eye itself.

VI

Nine months passed before the eye upon Oneness became
the eye upon nothingness. Without warning or reason, all
particulars dissolved into emptiness. At one point, the
mind came upon the hideous void of life, the insidious
nothingness of death and decay strangling life from every
object of sight. Only self can escape such a vision because
only self knows fear, and only fear can generate the weapons of defense. Without a self, the only escape is no
escape; the void must be faced — come what may. On
the hillside, the epitome of all that is dreadful and insane
was confronted — but who, or what beheld this terror?
And who or what could endure it? In the absence of self,
all that remained was an immovable stillness, an unbreak-
able, unfeeling silence. Would it move — crack open? Or
would it hold? This could not be known, surmised, or
even hoped for. What would be, would be.

VII

The stillness held fast because nothingness and emptiness cannot know fear or dread. Yet the wildflower yielded, gave way, expanded infinitely, to reveal a great intensity that could now be seen without the eye growing dim or the light going out. The body dissolves and melts into the stillness of what remains. Afterwards, the eye no longer sees anything at all. Instead, it presses downward on the mind like a terrible taskmaster demanding that it "See!" The mind can no longer focus on anything in particular or in general; it can see nothing within or without. It is in a state of complete unknowing, a dire state and a Passageway wherein, for months, the mind is fixed in a rigid now-moment out of which it cannot move, and in which there is nothing to see.

VIII

In this Passageway, true life, unlocalized and nowhere, reveals itself as that which remains and knows no death. It is this life that continues despite unseeing and unknowing, an eternal life that, strangely, has no God as the object of vision. But how can ordinary life go on without the energies of self, and when true life has no such energies? How is it possible to stay in the flesh and in the ordinary mind when no life seems to lie therein? The only answer is time — time to grow accustomed, to acclimate, to learn all over again how to live with this new life. To do so, the self is nowhere to help, the mind does not know how, and the body keeps melting away.

IX

When the adjustment is made — but barely — the journey appears to be over. At first, the nothingness of existence becomes endurable; later, it is an ordinary sight;
and finally, it is so taken for granted it is never noticed or
seen again. When nothing moves in to take its place,
nothingness becomes all that is; and this had, finally, to
be accepted as the most obvious of ultimate truths. Here it
could be clearly seen that all the searching, speculating,
and experiencing of a lifetime had been a gigantic waste —
a head-trip of such proportions that only the infant mentality can bare such a truth: the end is like the beginning,
and everything in between is pure deception. The state of
unknowing is permanent; since the mind can hold on to
no content, there is nothing more that can be learned.
There will be no more journeys; this is the last, the end
— an end which is absolute nothingness.

X

As the river flows, a smile emerges, and out of nothingness arises the greatest of great realities, more real than
anything that can be seen or known — yet, explicable only
in such terms. *The smile itself, "that" which smiled, and
that at which it smiled were identical.* This was the great
reality. The relative mind cannot hold, grasp, convey,
see, or even believe, that which has revealed itself. This
identity can never be communicated because it is the one
existent that is Pure Subjectivity, and can never be objectified. This is the Eye seeing itself, and wherever it looks
it sees nothing but itself.

XI

Later, after its four-month absence, the Oneness reappeared, but no longer through a medium (the particular);
it was "there" — everywhere. But its return was too late;
something had now been seen and known, compared to
which, all else was but a deception. Still, the mind
wanted to look at it, it *had* to look, and when it did, the
Oneness vanished and instantly the mind understood
why. It understood what it meant, how it worked, and
what still remained to be done. After a long passage, the
mind had finally come to rest and rejoice in its own understanding. Now it was ready, prepared, to take its
rightful place in the immediacy and practicality of the
now-moment. No more searching, looking, retaining; no
need to know that which it understands it can never
know. And in this state of unknowing, the mind is content to dwell forever. The Eye — which is not of the
mind — alone sees and knows itself as all that exists; it *is*
Oneness, and it *is* itself all that remains when there is no
self.

XII

Yet another period of acclimating, of adjusting to the
non-relative life beyond the Passageway. Then, just as the
self had once faded into silence, so too, the silence and
stillness of no-self faded beyond recognition. The journey
— its experiences, insights, and learning devices — had
only been the means of transition from the old to the new
life, from a relative to a non-relative way of knowing and
seeing. It was over now; the gap between subject and object had been irrevocably closed. Beyond the relational
there is only the Eye seeing itself, which is not static;
rather, it sees itself as so continuously new, that the now-
moment is never the same. Since the movement into the
new is of its essence, the journey moves on, endlessly on-
ward into the Unknown.

How It Works

That which remains when there is no self is what Is.
There is no multiplicity of existences; only what Is has existence, an existence that can expand itself into an infinite variety of forms that constitute the movement and manifested aspect of itself.

Though what Is, is the act, movement, and changing of all forms — and is form itself — it is, at the same time, the unchanging, unknowable aspect of all form. Thus, that which Is, continually observes the coming and going — the changing and movement — of its own form or acts, without participating in any essential change itself.

Since the nature or essence of Itself is act, there can be no separation between its knowing, acting, existing, or between any aspect of itself, because *that which acts, that which it acts upon, and the act itself are one without division.* It never goes outside itself to know itself because the unmanifested, the manifesting, and the manifested are One.

The form of what Is is sustained as if there were a tension between its existence and its act that cannot be separated, because the very intensity or tension of this act is the nature and essence of Itself.

Since what Is is an undivided whole, no single manifestation or form can know the totality of itself. This completeness can only be known when the manifested falls back into the unmanifested, or when the tension is released between act and being — as a sunburst that retracts its ray back into itself.

O

All that man knows of God, or what Is, is either theoretical — and therefore speculative — or is no more than one man's attempt to describe his experience of "that" which is all that Is.

The Silent Mind

I wish I understood the mechanism of self-consciousness, or how it is possible for the mind to bend back on itself, for if I did, I could more easily convey a better understanding of no-self and its most noticeable effect — the silent mind. But whatever this mechanism is, the state of no-self is the breaking up of a self-conscious system whereby the mind can no longer see itself as an object; and at the same time it loses the ability to find any other object to take its place, because when there is no self there is also no other.

I might add that the mind has never had the ability to see itself as subject — this would be as impossible as the eye seeing itself; yet I think this very impossibility may be the clue to the type of consciousness that remains when consciousness without a knowable subject or object becomes the whole of it. This type of consciousness is not available to our ordinary way of knowing, and because it cannot be experienced or understood by the relative mind, it falls squarely into the realm of the unknown and the unknowable.

I used to believe that in order to know of the self's existence, it was not necessary for the mind to reflect back on itself — to make itself an object or to be self-conscious, that is; instead, I believed that the basic awareness of thoughts and feelings went right on, and was present whether I reflected on them or not. Now, however, I see this is not the way it works. I see this is an error, but an error it is only possible to realize once self-consciousness had come to an end. It seems that on an unconscious level this reflexive mechanism goes on so continuously, it makes no difference if we are aware of this mechanism on a conscious level or not. In turn, this means that when the mechanism is cut off, we not only lose awareness of the self — or the agent of consciousness on a conscious level — but we lose awareness of the self on an unconscious level as well. Stated more simply: *when we can no longer verify or check back (reflect) on the subject of awareness, we lose consciousness of there being any subject of awareness at all.* To one who remains self-conscious, of course, this seems impossible. To such a one, the subject of consciousness is so evident and logical, it needs no proof. But to the unself-conscious mind, no proof is possible.

The first question to be asked is whether or not self-consciousness is necessary for thinking, or if thinking goes right on without a thinker. My answer is that thinking can only arise in a self-conscious mind, which is obviously why the infant mentality cannot survive in an adult world. But once the mind is patterned and conditioned or brought to its full potential as a functioning mechanism, thinking goes right on without any need for a self-conscious mechanism. At the same time, however, it will be a different kind of thinking. Where before, thought had been a product of a reflecting introspective, objectifying mechanism — ever colored with personal feelings and biases — now thought arises spontaneously off the top of the head, and what is more, it arises in the now-moment which is concerned with the immediate present, making it invariably practical. This is undoubtedly a restrictive state of mind, but it is a blessed restrictiveness since the continual movement inward and outward, backward and forward in time, and in the service of feelings, personal projections, and all the rest, is an exhausting state that consumes an untold amount of energy that is otherwise left free.

What this means is that thinking goes right on even when there is no self, no thinker, and no self-consciousness; thus, there is no such thing as a totally silent mind — unless, of course, the mind or brain (which I view as synonymous) is physically dead. Certainly something remains when the mind dies, but this "something" has nothing to do with our notions or experiences of a mind, or of thought, or of ordinary awareness.

What I call a "silent mind," therefore, is a purely relative experience belonging to a self-conscious state wherein silence is relative to its absence, its opposite, or to some degree of mental quietude. But in a fully established non-relative state — which is non-experiential by ordinary standards — there are no longer the variations, degrees, or fluctuations that could be known as a silent mind. This does not mean we cannot pass beyond the mind to "that" which remains when self-consciousness falls away, but it does mean that whatever lies beyond the mind has no such tool for its description.

One way to look at this journey is to see it as a process of acclimation to an unself-conscious mind, or as a transition from a relative to a non-relative way of knowing. But however we care to regard it, the fact remains that the initial, most noteworthy effect of the falling away of the reflexive mechanism is a silent mind. This means that the silent aspect of the mind is actually the absence of self, or as I prefer to call it — the silence of no-self.

Ordinarily it never occurs to the mind how completely subjective it is, or how automatically and unconsciously every thought, word, and deed is filtered through a self-conscious mechanism. Thus, when the door upon the self is closed, we seem at first to be in an unusual state; but because everything appears as usual, we are at a loss to say what has changed. We know something is missing but cannot put our finger on it. When this happens, or when the subject can no longer see itself, it feels lost to itself and begins groping around for some object of mind to fill the old need. Yet of itself and by its own efforts, the objectless mind is powerless to do this because no other object will come in to view or arise to take its place.

It would seem then, there is a step beyond no-self which is the objectless seeing of what Is; and each of these steps, namely, the coming upon no-self, and the eventual seeing of what Is, has a type of silence peculiar to itself. It is these two types of silence — especially the former — I would like to focus on because they are like no other types of silence I had come upon, or could hold on to, prior to taking this journey.

To start with, it may be helpful to draw a comparison between man's basic mental structure and that of a dry sponge; a sponge which is light and airy can easily be carried along by the breezes that come its way. If, however, we take the sponge and saturate it in the waters of selfhood, it becomes heavy, ponderous, and bloated, and because it cannot respond to the breezes, it goes virtually nowhere. If, somehow, such a sponge can stay away from these waters and no longer allow itself to be used, it will eventually, by sitting alone and aloof for a long time, dry out and return to its original structure. But there's another way this can happen. This is for an outside agent to pick up the sponge and squeeze it dry — quickly and all at once — then put it aside to be used for other purposes than the absorbing of water.

The sponge that has been quickly dried has, at first, a unique sense of emptiness and freedom. It takes a while to adjust to a new way of life wherein it eventually discovers that the basic structure of the mind and its faculties remain intact and perfectly functional, but functional in a new way, a way no longer weighed down by the absorption of water. Although it knows there has been some radical change that seems to be a transformation into something other than what it was, in time it sees it has only returned to what it was originally; and thus, everything seems to be the same as before, with the only difference being the absence of the waters of self.

If we could fully realize how every cell of the mind is saturated with the waters of self continually oozing outward (projecting) and seeping inward (absorbing), we might have some idea of what it would be like if all such movements came to an end. Once the mind can no longer reflect on itself, all energy or movement of the self is gone; the feelings and emotions are in silence; the memory has been so denuded that the past is lifeless with no continuum at all. From here on, each small event becomes the totality of the moment, and when this moment is over, it too has no continuum. Introspection becomes impossible; and projection is also out of the question since we can no longer endow any object with the usual values, meanings, and purposes; nor can we touch upon objects when there is no water forthcoming to go outward.

Our ordinary frames of reference have disappeared, leaving an empty mind, and since the mind can hang onto nothing, it must remain in the darkness of its own un-understanding. Initially, it is not only the thinking powers of the mind that are silent, but it is every cell of the sponge that has been wrung out and must wait in emptiness for the breezes that will carry it along. Here we have encountered a mysterious, unique type of silence; and since it is not of the self, it is as nothing ever experienced before — it is the permanent silence of no-self.

Some people think that silencing the mind or the continual flow of thought is what it takes to be rid of the self. Perhaps Descartes would think so. If he can say, "I think, therefore I am" then it would also make sense to say, "If I don't think, therefore I am not." In reality, however, nonthinking produces mere nothingness. A silent mind is not a blank mind, rather it is a mind in which the reflex arc — or whatever it is that allows the self to become an object — has been broken in two, so that thinking goes right on, but now by-passes the synaptic self that continually colors incoming data before sending it out again. When this break occurs, it naturally eliminates a great deal of thought and thinking, but only that which was constricting and irrelevant in the first place. As said before, the thoughts that now come to mind do not arise from within, but originate "off the top," so to speak, and then, only when dealing with the obvious data at hand at any given time.

Initially it could be said that "doing" replaces thought, because when we listen, talk, read, or work, we are (at first) accompanied by a mysterious silence, which is nothing more than the relative absence of a functioning self-conscious mechanism. In this way the mind is always clear, but not clear of thought *per se*, only clear of thought that had been clouded and infected by the waters of self.

Once I had come upon the silence of no-self, I recognized it as a coming together of various types of silences I had experienced earlier in life. As a way of clarifying this state and making it more recognizable, I would like to recount several of these experiences because at some time or other, everyone has undoubtedly touched upon no-self.

Fleeting moments of this state occurred off and on beginning at the age of six or thereabouts. Lying in the bow of my father's boat, my body in tune with the roll of the sea and my mind absorbed in the rhythmic splash of the water, I felt I had gently and quietly dissolved, and all that remained was a small, weightless cork, floating aimlessly and contentedly in a vast, endless sea. The hustle and bustle of life had come to an end, and despite the continuation of sound and motion there was a mysterious silence and stillness in the atmosphere which could not be accounted for; perhaps it was just the peace and quiet joy of the elements themselves. I could have remained this way forever...when suddenly an arm was thrust out of the porthole with a hotdog in hand. It was a rude awakening, a gesture I could not, for a moment, understand; it appeared out of place and harsh by comparison. But of one thing I was certain: all that appeared to be, including myself, was not all there was, because there was something around that was better — and I determined then to find it.

In searching for this experience, I discovered that while I could not make it happen, I could nevertheless put myself in situations conducive to its recurrence and thus, alone and out of doors, lying on the grass under a tree in the hills, or floating on the sea, I became acquainted with this experience which I now recognize as fleeting moments of no-self — moments that would one day be the whole of time. In retrospect, I also understand why, at that time, those foretastes could not have become a permanent state. The ground must first be prepared so there will be no rude awakenings or contrasts between what appears and what Is; and we come to this gradually by continually readjusting our lives in order to see deeper into what exists. Indeed, it takes a lot of living before no-self can become a permanent state.

About this same age, I came upon another type of silence, a silence I always referred to as my "blank mind." This was discovered while listening to the Lone Ranger on the radio — or when I finally decided the best thing about this program was its music. Whenever it was turned up (from the Ranger's end of it) I would put my ear to the speaker to let the music empty my mind, free me from my surroundings, and drown me in its tones. Later I discovered that when I tried to concentrate on a school lesson or a difficult math problem, my mind would again gravitate to this same blank state. Finally I discovered I could "go blank" anytime I wanted to. In this way, I learned how to tune out the world and become free at will.

I found this mental silence strangely attractive, intriguing, and mysterious. It seemed to exert a forcible pull downward, down into an abyss of darkness and silence that had varying degrees and levels. I used to wonder how far down it went, or if there was an end to it, and what would happen if I went all the way. On one occasion I discovered what would happen, and in so doing, met up with a frightening possibility.

I was eleven at the time, and finding myself in a boring classroom, decided to put my head down on the desk and go blank. But as soon as I did this, I knew I had sunk in further than ever before because the emptiness was so complete I seemed to lose all memory of myself. At first I tried to visualize what I was wearing that day and when this failed, I tried to remember getting up in the morning and the faces of my parents at the breakfast table, but when this couldn't be done I tried to remember my own face, and when this proved impossible, I put my hand on my head to be sure it was still there. In doing so, I noticed my arm felt like a dead weight and realized that my physical energy had been drained by this silence which now appeared heavy and oppressive. Suddenly I was afraid I would never be able to move out of this silence again — never be able to remember myself — and with one thrust of sheer panic I leaped out of the seat and began taking deep breaths to get back a sense of myself.

After this I vowed never to go blank again, yet sometimes the forceful pull inwards, to drop into this unknowable silence, was so strong I had to get up, run, or do something to divert its influence. There was nothing spiritual about this blank mind; I never connected it with a thing except to blame it for all my stupidity, because I was convinced it prevented me from developing a profound thinking mind. As soon as the questions became too profound, I would not only go blank but forget the questions as well. I had a poor memory and seemingly no imagination since it was impossible to retain visual pictures without mental strain.

Nevertheless, in time I lost my fear of a blank mind and in the end, came to regard it as a blessing in disguise that served me well throughout life. This is a type of silent mind in which self can be lost from view, and on this journey, it was this silence of no-self that became a permanent state. It goes without saying that I could not have lived in this state at an earlier age, the developmental process alone would not have allowed it. As said before, there was yet a lot of living to be done.

At the age of fifteen I discovered yet another type of silence, a silence that was not of the mind and not that of the little cork which was at one with its environment, but a silence at the inner core of my being which I called the "still-point." Before taking this journey, I looked upon the self as the totality of my existence — body and soul, mind and feelings — it was everything but the central axis about which it moved or revolved. Compared to everything outside this center, the still-point appeared to be still, unmovable, permanent, silent, and utterly peaceful. It was the source of joy and great energy, and once I realized it was God, I went after it and decided to embark upon a contemplative vocation.

This type of silence can spread outward (or possibly draw inward) to engulf the faculties of mind and emotions to such an extent that, at times, all that remains of the self appears to be the still-point Itself. But here too, the experiences were impermanent, and after two years the still-point vanished, leaving a black, bottomless hole at the center of my being.*

I was fortunate, however, in having the only help I was to find in my life in the person of a Carmelite priest I had known for several years. His joy over this darkness seemed proportionate to my misery, for he had this theory that the lower you go, the higher you rise — "like a ball," he said. Thus, with his encouragement I sat still, gritted my teeth, and took all the pain I could, hoping against all conceivable odds he was right about this whole thing. I might add that the pressure behind the eyes, spoken of during the Passageway, was also at work here; evidently it is the herald of a new type of seeing.

After the Dark Night, the type of silence I met was like the great calm after a storm.

But increasingly it occurred to me that it was all too natural — as if it were part and parcel of my own being and not at all from God. Eventually this gave rise to the idea that I was nothing more than a Quietist since there was nothing *in* this silence, only silence itself. These fears grew disturbing, until I finally met someone who assured me this silence was a grace for which I should be grateful, and if I gave no space to these fears, they would disappear — which eventually proved to be true.

This silence, however, is not a silence of the mind, but a coming upon the permanent accessibility to the still-point that can always be seen, and into which the self can descend or dissolve through varying levels and degrees of silence. This was ever a joy and on-going refuge from the troubled waters that often surged overhead, for the still-point is a place of peace and imperturbability, lying deep below the surface of life's events and surroundings. Though I would often wonder where my silence left off and God's began, I eventually found enough troubles in life to just be glad we were "there" — and let the devil take the rest.

This is not the place to describe these various levels of interior silence, but in passing I would say that the pattern of all transient experiences is to act as a foretaste of a permanent state that lies a step ahead. Thus, when we first come upon a silent mind — or any other type of silence — it is a new and unusual event, but one to which we imperceptibly adjust while the next step is being revealed. In this way, what appears transient in the beginning will gradually, in the end, become a permanent state. This explains why no two experiences are alike, and why they never repeat themselves. It also explains how life is a continual movement, and why the contemplative is one who is aware of this movement.

The present journey, or second contemplative move-

ment as I have called it, was a coming together of every
type, level, and degree of silence that had ever been experienced; at the same time, it was the end of all such experiences. In retrospect, it is possible to understand the nature
of these silences as the stilling of the self, a step-by-step
movement or entry into the irreversible and permanent state
of no-self. It seems that from the day we are born, or from
the day the self begins to develop, we are getting ready for a
life without a self. It is as if the mechanisms of self-preservation and self-extinction are living in balance, and guiding us
to our true destiny. And if the former predominates in the
first half of life, it is the latter that comes to fore in the second
half, wherein no-self becomes the true, preserving force.

What this means is that all our experiences of silence
are nothing more, yet nothing less, than the silence of no-
self — a mysterious foretaste of what is yet to be. It means
the waters of self are gradually being wrung from the structure of being; that the mechanism of self-consciousness is
coming to an end in a way we may never understand. And
above all, it means that without a self we are free to come
upon that which lies beyond any notion or experience of
silence. No-self is not God; rather, it is the gap between self
and God, and the gateway to what is not only beyond the
self, but beyond no-self as well.

So here, the first movement is the transition from self
to no-self, while the second movement is the transition from
no-self to nowhere — meaning nowhere in particular, yet
everywhere in general. It is a transition from a relative
silence to the non-relative silence of what Is, and if I call the
latter a silence it is because no words can be used for description. It can be known, however, known as it knows Itself; what Is, knows not words nor does it communicate as
such.

Once the journey was ended, I discovered the increas-
ing ability to sustain more fully the great intensity, without
the light going out — that is, without going unconscious,

blacking out, or dropping into a consciousless darkness in which there is nothing at all. Thus, there came the necessary strength to bear the vision with full consciousness. In doing so, the awareness of everything else falls away — the body, surroundings, the silence, everything — and compared to this intensity, the loss of self is as nothing, for man, indeed the whole universe, has far more to lose than itself.

The step beyond no-self is like the dissolution of that which remains when It draws back into Itself as if overcome by its own intensity. Even though what Is, is all that Is, its acts (or doing), which is identical with itself, is not its entirety; what we ordinarily know of it is only that which falls into the realm of the known. But there seems to exist a fullness of act that does not fall into the known, and to be overcome by this fullness means that at any moment all we know to exist may easily, instantly, and painlessly be dissolved into what Is. I do not understand this mechanism, but I do know that this dissolution, this enduring of intensity, is the ending and the last of all silences.

---

* In this way I entered the great Dark Night of the Soul, a night of terrible psychological pain—a burning out of the faculties of mind and will, which lasted nine months without let-up.

Part II   A Closer Look

Questions and Comments

After several friends read this account, I realized the necessity of clarifying certain aspects of the journey's events. For one person at least, the complaint referred to gaps in the transition between one phase of the journey and another.

To give an example of this, I was asked what explanation I could give for the seeing of Oneness suddenly turning into the seeing of emptiness. At the time, of course, I had no explanation — which was half the problem — and even now I can only conjecture that it was part and parcel of the transition from a relative to a non-relative type of perception, wherein I had been given so much time to see how every object faded into the same identical Oneness before it became necessary to see Oneness directly and immediately, without going through the medium of objects or individual form. It seems that as long as we can still see Oneness, we continue to live and perceive on a relative plane, which means we are still able to see no Oneness, or its opposite — such as the horrible void I saw on the beach. In other words, as long as God is an object to be observed — even a formless "something" — we are still on a relative plane and, therefore, just as likely to come upon no God or no such object. Why? Because God cannot be seen with the relative mind or with a subject-object type of consciousness.

What this means is that prior to the Great Passageway,

and with the help of the 3D glasses, I was still able to switch back and forth from a relative to a non-relative type of perception, or to see Oneness as well as individuality. Once beyond the Passageway, however, there was no seeing of either Oneness or individuality, but only the seeing of what Is, which is beyond the relative plane, and therefore beyond even the One and the many. Thus, on a strictly non-relative plane, what Is is the Eye seeing itself, and wherever it looks it sees only itself.

O

Another point to clarify is that the seeing of emptiness is not the seeing of world-as-illusion. For me, emptiness and illusion have no relationship; in fact, I am not sure what an illusion is because I doubt I have ever seen one. My own notion of an illusion is that it is merely an error in perception, which I now see — in retrospect — goes on as long as self is coloring the world as something it is not. Compared to a non-relative reality, all our thoughts about the real are illusions of a sort, but until we "see," we have no way of knowing this, and therefore have no way of recognizing an illusion. Once beyond the self, however, we see our illusions in retrospect and realize they were only what we *thought* about reality; thoughts which had nothing to do with the real world of objects and forms as they are in themselves. I see the world and its contents as utterly real, even though the contents have no individual existence of their own, but are part of One reality, One existent. At the same time, I recognize that all form is fragile, subject to change, and may easily and quickly dissolve into the Oneness from which it came; but none of this is an illusion. Nevertheless, I think I may know where the notion of world-as-illusion is coming from, or where it originates on a purely experiential basis.

By the end of the journey, there is no longer the perceptual ability to focus on the particular, or individual, because the state of consciousness is such that what Is becomes the only reality seen everywhere. It's almost like looking at the world through a veil so that objects are no longer clearly defined. This is a reversal of the type of perception given by the 3D glasses whereby form gave way to Oneness; because here, at the end of the journey, Oneness is seen first, before it gives way to form. Consequently the veil grows thicker every day and the distinctness of form grows proportionately dim and faded.

The day I can no longer see anything through the veil, or see anything else but Oneness — when there is no form left to see — I too will be gone, dissolved, as all form will, into what Is. In the meantime, I cannot regard the continual coming and going of my children as the interruptions of mere illusion — though I admit it would be helpful, at times, if this could be done.

O

Another point that arose in the course of the reading was the impression that I was often in a daze of unreality, a dream-like state perhaps, or a state of bewilderment and confusion. Such, however, was not the case; nor did anyone suspect anything unusual going on. And had I told them, they would not have understood. A religious friend said he was amazed when he read the account because he had no idea, despite our frequent discussions, that anything of this nature or intensity was in process. There were no personality changes, no illnesses and, apart from a number of memory failures, there were no atypical behaviors. In a word, no one judged me to be anything but my usual self. To account for this, I can only say that the preparation must have been right: by temperament, an extreme realist; by profession, a mother; by the grace of God, a contemplative; put together, these somehow got me through. Then too, from earliest childhood I was familiar with the ways of God, and never doubted these events were of His doing. Even at the end of the Passageway, when confronted with the rock-bottom, absolute nothingness of existence, I was convinced that this truth, this nothingness, had led me to this end because, for me, truth and God were synonymous. I trusted this truth, however it cared to reveal itself at any given moment.

But if, on a practical level, there was no mental confusion, on the impractical or intellectual level, I was indeed surprised and bewildered by events I did not understand. Yet, when the mind lives solely in the now-moment — which is akin to a state of unknowing — it becomes incapable of disorder and confusion, for the now-moment deals only with the real, the actual, and the practical. In contrast, it is the continuous, unsettled movements of the mind in a state of knowing that are solely capable of giving rise to indecision, confusion, unreality, and so on.

O

When it comes to maintaining psychic balance on a journey of this nature, time is yet another important factor. I cannot believe it is possible to acclimate in a single day to the falling away of the self, since the change of consciousness that ensures this entails a revamping of every aspect of our life — the mind, the feelings, the perceptions, down to physical sensations. Apart from certain memory (or time) lapses, I was not impressed with any sense of timelessness, unless of course, this means living without clock and calendar, which I did in the mountains; this proved interesting, but nothing more. If anything, I was impressed that this change took time and that time itself seems to be the essence of life's movement. I cannot say the ultimate reality is timeless; I can only say it has its own time. This factor then, may have been responsible for the ability to take the journey in stride, since the now-moment moves forward imperceptibly, but dynamically nonetheless.

O

In some ways, the fact that I myself always appeared so completely ordinary may have worked to my disadvantage when, on occasion, I went in search of help and found that no one could take me seriously. I wasn't a monk or a nun; I didn't practice a thing; I had no charisma and exuded no light. I was a woman basically geared to a teenage milieu. In a word — I inspired no one. According to one Zen monk, the reason I had to have a self was because I was not omniscient and omnipresent. Since this is the Christian notion of God, I thought he was joking and laughed heartily, only to discover he was in earnest, because this is indeed the Buddhist notion of someone who no longer has a self! Evidently I was in the wrong camp — but how did he know? I think he was only telling me I was just too unspectacular, too ordinary, and too common to have come upon no-self.

This reply was in keeping with another comment made by a friend who said that for her, at least, the ending of the journey was a letdown, because after all the sound and fury, the final seeing was so ordinary and unspectacular, it was difficult to appreciate by comparison. I could understand this comment; after all, how many can honestly appreciate the triumph of being common? Who can understand what it means to learn that the ultimate reality is not a passing moment of bliss, not a fleeting vision or transfiguration, not some ineffable, extraordinary experience or phenomenon but instead, is as close as our eyes, as simple as a smile, and as clear as the identity of "that" which remains when there is no self? The expectation of the grand finale being one of love and bliss is a failure to realize that such responses are the responses of self to an object — the experiences of a self — while what Is does not respond to itself as an object or in similar fashion. On the contrary, it can be said that the Eye sees itself as "usual," just as it "ordinarily" does all the time, and is a "common" sight wherever it looks. If we had been

looking at ourselves all our lives, at what point would we go
into ecstasy upon seeing ourselves? It may only be deceiving
to think the ultimate reality is love and bliss since such experiences may have nothing to do with God at all. As said
before, I am convinced we continually see this Reality all
our lives but do not recognize it because it is so usual, common, and ordinary that we go off in search of more tantaliz-
ing experiences — experiences more gratifying to the self.
Thus, when we can look in the mirror and not experience
the great disappointment, but can say instead, "everything
is as usual and nothing has changed" then, perhaps, we shall
know the intense triumph of being common.

O

Another comment concerned the notion of "doing,"
which a friend thought could easily be construed as a need
to keep busy, occupied, or even, become a workaholic.
Though I hope this impression was not conveyed, I see the
need for clarification if it is thought to mean the changing
from a contemplative to a more altruistic or active way of
life. But these are already compatible, if not identical, ways
of living. For a better understanding, it might be helpful to
contrast the notion of "doing" to John of the Cross' notion
of the "perfect act," which is an act undertaken by anyone
who has attained the state of union with God. In this case,
such an act is a perfect act of love no matter what the act is
in itself. It could be a prayer, a household chore, or a sharing and concern for others. It is a doing for the sake of love,
and prompted by energies created by a union that must find
expression in an outward flow. At the close of the first, or
earlier, contemplative journey, I came upon this type of
energy and act, but it is not the same act or doing I speak of
here.

In the present movement there are no such energies;
there is nothing within to go out, and nothing without to

reach for. There is no longer even a union of love, because when there is no self, there is nothing left to be united. Here it is discovered that God is a whole, whose acts cannot be divided or separated from his existence. Thus from here on, to act is to do so unconsciously, because it is your very nature to act and you cannot do otherwise. What is more, there is no self to get into the act because self *was* the energy formerly experienced — it *was* the doer. But without a self (doer), act is identical with existence.

The notion of doing is difficult to convey because we usually think of it in terms of a doer, of doing "something," or of "what" we do, but all this is the content of doing, and is a divisive factor we are not ordinarily aware of until there is no self, and no content remaining. So, when there is no longer any separation between act and being, then there is doing.

O

Purely on the surface, I have noticed a great similarity between the first and second contemplative movements. Some twenty-five years ago I wrote about the first journey, and in looking over my notes I noticed that the final chapter was entitled "Doing, not Being" (obviously, still a division between doing and being), in which there was an overwhelming need to vent the energies created by a newly discovered oneness with God. But before coming upon the notion of doing — at the end of the first journey — I had undergone a severe trial and a certain loss of self (dissimilar from the present journey) that seemed, for a time, to culminate in a deadend when, suddenly, something burst in upon me and I "see." At the end of the first journey, I saw how God was the Eternal Movement which I must follow if I were not to thwart the burning force encountered by a love I could not contain. It was a love that wanted to move outward either to share with others, find creative expression or, if nothing else, become a test of endurance — which was the path I was destined to take.

Yet despite these similarities, the end was not the same because the journey was not the same. In the early years, there had been a struggle between nature and grace that eventually disappeared into a powerful sense of wholeness that had to move outward — as a unit, not as a fragmented, scattered force — because now, the energies of self were in tune with the Eternal Movement. While the second journey also ended with a sense of wholeness, it was a wholeness of "that" which remains when there is no self and no God for the self. Here, no energies are forthcoming to go out; instead there only remains the intensity of act, the act of sheer living, the living of a nature so intelligent as to be incomprehensible and inaccessible to the conscious mind.

I regard the second movement as a continuation and completion of the first, and look upon the intervening years as the test of endurance, or necessary proving-ground, before the onset of the second journey. There is a tendency, I believe, to confuse these two movements if they are regarded as basically identical, or when the only difference seen is one of interpretation — particularly the interpretation of the end. It is thought that union with God either by "participation" or "identification" is merely a difference of theological concern, whereas each of these notions is actually the culmination of two separate movements. I think the reason for this misunderstanding is due to the inadequacy of the accounts recorded; or because these accounts were not sufficiently personal or detailed to fill the gap between theory and practice. The second movement is not well known or understood, and the reason is not difficult to surmise.

To journey beyond the self means leaving behind our relative notions, expectations, and theories concerning what lies beyond the known. It means going beyond our usual frames of reference and encountering areas of theological sensitivity which, alone, would necessitate such accounts remaining unrecorded. I have always been of the opinion that John of the Cross, with the Spanish Inquisition breathing down his neck, failed to give us the full story. We know that his writings were left incomplete.

O

In keeping with this, I was asked why, with the falling away of my Christian contemplative frame of reference, I did not seek help from other religious or philosophical traditions? The answer is that I did, indeed, search for other life-preservers, but I was never destined to make the right contact. I was not familiar with the Eastern disciplines and found the terminology alone, quite foreign. I couldn't get hold of the importance of reincarnation, karma, illusion, and had no understanding of the self they call Atman. It may sound easy to change directions in midstream, but I don't see how it is possible when you've gone this far. When you hit the rapids is not the time to step out and study the structure or soundness of various life-preservers that may or may not tame the stream for you. Furthermore, it seems the very nature of the crossing is an unhinging of every idea or belief we cling to regarding the structure of the world, the self, and God; an unhinging for which there are no substitutes, no life-preservers and no changing in midstream.

If I had any life-preserver at all it was nature itself, for in my most dire moments of total void, the fantastic design of my peacock friend was set up as the toughest contradiction to an unknowing mind. Every morning as we ate our cereal — often from the same bowl — I knew: although every intellectual and theological expectation had been smashed against the rocks of a reality they could not penetrate, the plumage of this friend by my side stood in opposition to all notions of void or chance. But the simple and obvious evidence of an ingenious artist at work could not penetrate my mind because I could not "see" and knew I couldn't. Thus, faced with this intense contradiction, I sometimes put down the bowl for him to finish and turned away. In other words, I saw, but could not see.

Early in the journey, while reading a book by Thomas Merton, a Christian contemplative monk, I came across the Buddhist's notion of no-self and followed up this important discovery by reading several books in this philosophical frame of reference. Reading books, however, will never lend verification for an experience outside their own frame of reference. Therefore, to seek more understanding and clarification, I spent a week at a Zen Monastery where I told them, in all honesty, I had come to find out how I might ascertain — according to their own tradition — if I had any self left or not. I also asked them to please explain to me what remained when the self was gone. My questions must have seemed naïve to them for the silence I met with seemed to indicate these questions were a monastic taboo. There was no discussion, no explanation, no answers, and consequently, no help.

Once again I was forced back upon my own resources, which were growing scantier every day. In all fairness, however, I admit to meeting a similar silence when, shortly before this journey began, I sent a note to my Hermit friends telling them I would give a dollar to any monk who could tell me where self left off and God began. Needless to say, I didn't lose a penny on this inquiry because there wasn't a single taker. Without a doubt, when her time comes, every woman must go it alone.

O

Perhaps the only philosophy or theology that can help us cross the stream is one that admits: when you have learned it all and lived it thoroughly, then you had better get ready to have it all collapse when you discover the highest wisdom is that you know nothing. It is said that St. Thomas Aquinas, after writing his masterful tomes on Christian theology, suddenly had an experience of God that so silenced his mind that ever after, he never wrote a single word. In other words, St. Thomas literally fell outside his own frame of reference when he came upon "that" which no mind can comprehend nor pen describe. But now we are all stuck with these tomes, tomes that cannot enable us to see what he saw, and to which we cannot cling if we are to do so. It seems that ultimately we must go beyond all frames of reference when the Cloud of Unknowing descends, and all the thrashing around looking for a life-preserver won't do a bit of good.

Nevertheless, I now see a possible line of travel that may be of use before crossing the stream. It would be to start with the Christian experience of self's union with God, whereby we lose the fear of ever becoming lost — since we can only get lost in God. This is done with the help of Christ, the ever-present guru or master who, unlike other mediums, is always around when you need Him, in the stillness within or in the silence of the Eucharist without.

But when the self disappears forever into this Great Silence, we come upon the Buddhist discovery of no-self, and learn how to live without anything we could possibly call a self, and without a frame of reference, as we come upon the essential oneness of all that is.

Then, finally, we come upon the peak of Hindu discovery, namely: "that" which remains when there is no self is identical with "that" which Is, the one Existent that is all that Is.

I am not a scholar of religion East or West, and though I know each religion feels it can ford the stream alone, I would think it far superior to ford it together, because it is a difficult stream to cross no matter how well the life-preservers are constructed. Theoretically, such an eclectic ap-

proach may be impossible, but after taking this journey, I
am convinced that on an experiential level this is the way it
goes — this is the way the stream flows.

O

Finally, I would briefly comment on a statement made
by an individual who was incensed at my calling this a "contemplative" journey, because from her point of view it was
nothing more than a psychotic head-trip. Since I am not a
psychologist, and apart from the fact that I could find nothing comparable to this journey in the psychiatric literature
available to me, I have no rebuttal to offer from this particular perspective. Meeting up with an unknown horror,
memory lapses, loss of self, and other events are not, for
that matter, outside the classic contemplative literature.
What I could not find in either literature, however, was a
completely sane, religious, comprehensible, step-by-step account of a total, irreversible change of consciousness —
which results when self-consciousness falls away. Nevertheless, the view of this journey as a psychotic event is not truly
disturbing because, for some, this view may be all they
know.

But what remains inconceivable is that: having been a
contemplative all my life, I should have suddenly fallen outside God's plan for me or outside his control. That the contemplative often walks the fine line, dangles over pits, and
touches upon unusual dimensions of psyche and soul, is all
part of this great adventure, part of coming upon the truth
of *what* God is. Those who go strictly by the books are only
living vicariously. Those who call a halt, at dogma and sen-
timent, or when the going becomes psychologically uncer-
tain or frightening, are probably not true contemplatives to
begin with. But whatever my ignorance of psychology, as a
contemplative I have done my homework and am familiar
with the literature in this, my field of interest. And it is for

this reason I regard the permanent loss of self-consciousness as a step in the contemplative life that has had little coverage; and later, I shall give my reason for saying this.

Earlier, I gauged the end of the journey to be a time when the relative difference between life with or without a self was no longer apparent. I would carry this further to include all relative aspects of the journey such as seeing, doing, the silent mind, and so on. These were insightful learning devices within the acclimating process, which outwore their usefulness once the newness of discovery had been sufficiently incorporated into an ordinary way of life. Though no longer of practical use, I wrote about these insights because they belong to this transition period which was — and I underscore — *a relative experience*; merely a journey from the old to the new life.

While it was in progress, I never thought of this as a journey or a transition *per se*; instead, the basic conviction was that of having to acclimate to a profound, irreversible change in the ordinary state of consciousness, as well as to a new way of seeing and knowing. Yet, it was a change that, in the end, became most ordinary in itself.

This period in the contemplative life is not easy to articulate and, possibly, this is one reason it has been lost to the records, which is no help for those who come upon this step and wonder why no one has said anything about it. We will always have with us those who speak to us from the "other side," but what we really need to know is what they went through personally, to get there.

Since everyone knows how to get as far as the stream (the subject of most contemplative literature), and since heaven (the other side) can take care of itself, what we need to know is something about the crossing itself. We need to articulate, describe, understand, and explore the passage as best we can because, even if it will not help the man in midstream, at least he will know such a transition exists, and will not expect to wake up some morning to find himself on the opposite shore, fully adjusted to a new life — as if by some miracle. The only person I know who showed us this crossing by his personal example — and not by his words — was the man who ended his life on the cross. Christ never went out in a state of bliss because this isn't the way it happens; this isn't the road to the resurrection — to the new life. That it would take such a complete death to the self, even the greatest of selves is, as I see it, Christ's realistic message to all who would cross the stream.

O

When returning the manuscript, a friend asked me, "Now really, would you honestly recommend this journey to others?" I had to laugh; the use of the word "recommend" made the account sound like a sales pitch for a travel agency, wherein I was recommending everyone buy a ticket for what — to my friend, at least — was a most uncomfortable journey. As it stands, of course, the choice to make this passage or not to make it, is not ours. When it is time for departure — a time no man knows — this ship of life moves into new waters, and without a self, we have no say and no control. Then too, starting from different directions, we will each pass through a different terrain and set of events. We will each be going beyond a different self, so that the relative differences we notice along the way will not be the same; no two journeys can possibly be alike.

On the other hand, the word "recommend" is not terribly invalid, especially if we ask ourselves if Christ would recommend that we too be crucified. Or, whether we too are called to go to such lengths of selflessness in order to "see." Our answer will naturally depend upon the light in which we interpret Christ's death: did he give up his self so the rest of us would not have to do so? Or, did he give up his self to show us the lengths to which we must go in order to see?

Since it is not within my ability to explore the theological aspects of some possible answers, in the next chapter I will, nevertheless, give the answer I came upon at the end of the Passageway. For now, I will only say: yes, I would recommend this journey; not mine, of course, but any man's journey that would allow him to see "that" which lies beyond everything we can call a "self."

Where Is Christ?

Of those who read this account, one person regarded it as a Buddhist-type experience, another called it "pure Vedantic," while others saw it variously as an existential crisis, a middle-age syndrome, and in one case, a complete enigma. What struck me as curious, however, was that no one suggested it was a Christian experience — which, from beginning to end, was and still remains my only view of it.

I look upon it as that part of the Christian contemplative movement that found its ultimate resolve in no-self and the subjective "seeing" already discussed. Little has been written about this movement beyond the self; so little in fact that my search only recently came upon several pages in a book by Thomas Merton (New Seeds of Contemplation, pp. 282–285). For the most part, it seems contemplative authors take for granted that the more advanced soul goes no further when its interior life bursts into a flame of love, and it remains that way for the rest of its life — as if this were the end. Actually, it is only another beginning.

When I asked a religious friend why no one had seen this account in a more Christian light, he told me the Christian influence was not obvious because there were no references to scripture or to the teachings of the Church. I had, by my own acknowledgement, fallen outside the traditional frame of reference — or the beaten path of mystical theology so well traveled by Christian contemplatives. In a word, what happened to that hallmark of Christian revelation: where is Christ?

My immediate response to this question was a complete silence. But my second response is this: if understood correctly, the answer to this question is the key to the entire journey. If I'd had any assured answer to this question from the beginning, I don't see why I would have taken this journey in the first place. I was continually asking myself: what remains when there is no self? who or what sees Oneness? could God be the stillness within? could he be the terrible Taskmaster? and why, in the absence of self, had nothing moved in to take its place?

As an answer, Christ was not self-evident. God was not self-evident. Nothing was self-evident. This was a journey to the unknown, which is why it was so incomprehensible and why I bother to write about it. Yes, indeed, I too wanted to know: where is Christ?

Off and on during the journey, I wrote about Christ because I felt I was beginning to see him in a totally new light, beginning perhaps, to see as he had seen. Still, this notion lent no certitude. I could make no claim of duplicating his personal experiences when in fact, I didn't know them, and all I could do was to surmise. Nevertheless, I felt this certitude might be the clue to the entire journey and the final solution as well and in this, I was ultimately not mistaken. It was not until the end of the Passageway, however, that any sort of identification could be made, and it is this identification I would now like to discuss. Some background first, and a clearing up of two points in particular.

The first point regards a frame of reference. As I see it a reference is only as much as we know about any system of thought — in this case, religious thought. That which remains unknown or remains to be known, THAT to which all religions point, falls outside the system itself — as happens when faith shifts to seeing. In some way, everyman's experience of God falls outside a systematic way of knowing because the experience itself is beyond all that. I have often thought of Christ as one who fell outside his Jewish frame of reference when he saw the truth in it and went about setting the record straight. He had fulfilled the scriptures (done it all), realized its truth, and set out to open the eyes of others — those still within this frame of reference. Basically then, a reference is for those who do not see. With the onset of seeing, however, the frame of reference is seen in a totally new light wherein the old light pales by comparison and, sometimes, is seen as no longer applicable.

It is this possibility that makes the contemplative's path somewhat dangerous: he is continually beset by the fear of "falling out," abandoning too much, or being so honest with God, himself, and others, that he might possibly get thrown out. It's much easier to stay with the known, cling to our references, remain put and go nowhere. On the other hand, there are those who, from the outset, reject any and all frames of reference and these too, go nowhere. There is a difference between those who reject a system and those who eventually see the truth in it. But either way, a man can get lost, because this is the risk for those who accept or reject alike — but then, what is life without its risks?

I might add that it would be wholly misleading for a man who has crossed the stream to tell others that because all paths come to an end at the water's edge, they must therefore, reject any and every path they believe in. Certainly this is a premature and faulty insight. Since such a man denounces the very path he took himself, he unwittingly cuts himself off from those who come after — those he might wish to help. It were as if such a man had been handed a precious gift and told that if he used it wisely, he would obtain his greatest desire, and having used the gift and attained his objective, he buries it, instead of passing it along. Such an individual has somehow failed to see that the path that brought him to the stream is the same one that continues unseen and unrecognized over the waters. It is the

same path or gift that had promised him a safe crossing in
the first place. Everyone must make a beginning on some
path, one he believes will get him to the other shore when
his time comes; and this belief, this path or gift, is not nulli-
fied when the other side is reached, or when belief finally
yields to seeing.

The second point I wish to make refers to the absence
of scriptural quotations. I think it is obvious that this account was not *apropos* to the use of scripture. Like everyone else, of course, I could have made use of quotations, but
then, to what purpose? This is not a mystical treatise; I am
not a theologian or a mystic, or an official representative of
the Church. What is more, if there is anything in this account
contrary to scripture, I would not know how to respond.

Earlier in life, the Bible had often been a source of con-
solation and insight; at times, it described my experiences
better than I could have done for myself. Nevertheless, the
events in the present movement were more of an apocalyp-
tic adventure for which I had no mind at all. Like Job, I had
only to endure and wait, because neither history nor specific
words had any meaning to me. But more important perhaps, is the fact that the emphasis in my life was never really
on scripture; rather, it was on God's on-going communica-
tion and interior direction in the here and now. That this interior life eventually fell away, was only for the purpose of
entering a larger stream of life, a stream that took its own
course, wherein the search for direction is no longer of any
avail. On this journey, God no longer speaks or communi-
cates as such; it seems his final word is: "Be still, and see that
I am God."

I return now to the question: "Where is Christ?" I think
it is important to give some background before proceeding
to give the answer I came upon at the end of the Passageway. The reason for this background is to show how this
question had a precedence in my life long before the journey
began. Though baptized before I breathed and once again

after — just to be sure — and given the best Catholic education in home and school, I was nevertheless destined to have to struggle with Christ, a struggle of long duration wherein I continually sought a resolution that ever eluded any form of finality.

This struggle began with a playground incident when I was eleven. At that time, the "recess" rage was dodge-ball, but because I was on crutches I could not dodge. Yet I could throw so well that the final shots were always handed to me. Thus it turned out that every day the best two dodgers were left in the ring, and every day I hit them out. One day after a game, these two girls, who were sisters, came to me and said:

"You think you're hot stuff because your father is rich. Well, we've got news for you. Christ said it would be harder for a rich man to get into heaven than for a camel to get through the eye of a needle! He also said that the beggar Lazarus went to heaven and the rich man went to hell. . . ."

"Yeah," said her sister, "Christ loves the poor the most, you read the Gospels and you'll see this is true . . . he was poor himself . . . and said it was the poor who would inherit the kingdom of heaven. . . ."

"He also said you can't serve two masters at once," added the first sister. "You can't be rich and love God too . . . he came for the poor, not the rich. . . ."

I don't remember what else they said, but initially I wanted to assure them my dad owed money to Barker Brothers Furniture Store and that we were not rich — but they didn't give me a chance. The bell had rung, everybody was lining up, and all I got in was the last word: "I'll tell you one thing," I said. "I'd rather be rich and humble about it, than poor and proud of it — like you guys — because the proud aren't getting to heaven either!"

All that afternoon I occupied myself in class, thinking up rebuttals with which to slay my friends after school. But the more I thought about the issues they brought up, the angrier I became when I realized everything they had said was absolutely true. Christ had, in fact, come to save the poor, the oppressed, the sick, and the sinner, but since I was none of these things — how had he come for me? And what about others like me — my parents to name two — who were not poor, didn't suffer, and had never sinned? Why did Christ die for us; what was his special message to us? When I couldn't think of any answers, I decided to go to church after school and ask Christ directly.

The church was adjacent to school. To the right of the altar was a life-size crucifix from which Christ looked down with sorrowful glass eyes on anyone standing beneath.

Under this gaze I asked my questions, but barely got them out before a sense of some unknown tragedy swept over me like a wave that washed away my questions as if they didn't count, as if they were meaningless, childish. It was not a sense of pity or sorrow, but a sense of tragedy so profound as to be inexpressible and totally un-understand-able. Suddenly it occurred to me that maybe nobody really understood his death or even his message, and it was this, not his physical suffering, that was the real tragedy: nobody understood him! Though I wanted badly to understand what evidently had not been mentioned in the books, nothing came; the tragedy was impenetrable. I felt the door of my understanding was closed.

Finally I decided I had been taken in by a pair of glass eyes, and moved backward until I touched the pews behind. But the eyes followed, intently watching as if through their eyelids. To avoid this gaze, I went to the other side of the church, but here too the eyes were still watching. I found this exceedingly strange, even frightening, and thinking it might only be my imagination, I decided to move to the rear of the church, since I knew that if the eyes were still looking, I could not possibly see them from such a distance. This proved correct and I finally felt free to ask my questions. After doing so, I let my mind go blank to be sure the an-

swers would be his and not mine — but then, I had no answers so there was no fear on this score.

An hour must have gone by while I paced back and
forth across the rear of the church. No answers came; only
stubborn silence, a veritable blank wall. I grew impatient.
Surely these were not tough questions for God; he had all
the answers, so why would he keep this one from me?

Finally, it occurred to me: the reason he didn't answer
was because there *was* no answer. He couldn't tell me why
he had come for me because he hadn't come for me at all!
Many are called, but few are chosen, and I was not among
the few. Once again I was overtaken by a wave of profound
tragedy — he had in fact answered me from the beginning,
only I had not understood. Now I realized this was not *his*
tragedy, but my own, all mine — I had not been chosen!

For a moment I was as stunned and horrified as if I'd
been thrown out of heaven. The sense of being utterly lost
was indescribable. I thought I was about to be snuffed out,
when there arose in me a powerful burst of anger and out-
rage I could hardly contain. Immediately I left the church,
making sure to slam the huge door behind me.

For the first three blocks all I could think of was how
to break this news to the family, since I knew I would never
go back to church again. I didn't belong; to go would be
pure hypocrisy, and if they forced me, I might turn into a
pharisee! My father's ire would be hard to bear, but going
back to church would be worse than anything I could think
of. In conscience, I couldn't do it.

When I got to the fourth block, the scenery changed.
The street was lined with trees; glancing up I saw clouds
overhead, and at the sight of my old friends I almost cried, I
was so happy to see them. Nature, always so faithful, beautiful, and uplifting; always above the problems of life and
always "there" to help me! I stood awhile, looking up, to let
its mysterious detachment come over me, dissolve my problems, and restore a lost peace.

For a moment, I was reminded of an experience I had a year before, when the family had gone to the high Sierras for a picnic. While the others went for a hike, I roamed the forest on my crutches and eventually managed to climb atop a high boulder. For a fleeting moment, the surroundings gave way to an unknown immensity, to something that had no description because it was invisible, formless, and unlocalized; yet it seemed only to be passing. Whatever it was, I knew it hadn't touched me; I felt nothing and had been given no time to think. But once it passed, I felt a leap of joy that took me by surprise and instantly I knew what I had seen: it was God — finally I had seen him! I had no doubts, not then, not ever; but the joy could not be contained. It spread over the boulder, tumbled into the stream below, overflowed its banks and climbed the trees to the sky. It was an experience of a lifetime. Just its remembrance, and everything else would fall away as if it were nothing, absolutely nothing.

Though God had passed, the joy remained. I had only to look inside to see its traces. Yet I tried not to look because I felt toward it a certain skepticism. With its sudden appearance in the mountains, I recognized this leap-of-joy as an old friend that had deserted me in my illness the year before. It had refused to help me. In fact, it disappeared before my very eyes, and when this happened, I was so devastated even God could not have helped me. That time the sea had to cure me. For this reason I never wanted to depend on its mysterious presence: if things got tough, it might disappear again. But ignore it, I could not. Despite my caution, it not only persisted. I soon discovered it was a good detector of God's passing by. Without warning, it would suddenly leap, and I would dash out of doors to catch the traces of a great Immensity that had already gone by.

So, standing there looking skyward on this day of tragedy and anger, I thought to myself: since I've already seen God in the woods, who needs Christ? I can love God without him — despite him. In fact I don't need him at all! And there rose in me a great determination to love God, a determination proportionate to the necessity of doing so without Christ. He wouldn't help me, so I would go it alone. With this idea, I found much peace, even joy, and continued on my way.

After dinner that night, I decided to break the news to my father. Starting with the playground incident, I told him what I had learned in church, and ended by saying that despite all his fine desires, despite his having chosen for me, I was nevertheless not Christ's choice, and saw no way we could force his hand in this matter — man proposes but God disposes.

I need not recount my father's credentials and will only say that in matters of religion, few people were as knowledgeable. He knew as much about the Church, its theology, and teachings as any priest — in some areas even more — and added to this was a legal and philosophical mind that thrived in a milieu of discussion and debate. He would often say that a Christian who did not ask questions wasn't worth his salt. When angry, he could be quite dogmatic, but in discussion he was always fair and never once undermined my thinking powers; instead, he would have me push them to their limits. So this night there began a series of discussions that would only end with his death many years later.

The first item he went over was the various ways in which the notion of being "chosen" could be construed in a theological context. The next item, original sin, was to become a continuing thorn of contention and discussion which I will not go into. But this night, he left me with the challenge of trying to think up a better way to solve the problem of evil which, for the moment, I could not do. This led us to the redemption and the meaning of Christ's life and death, followed by a discussion on the true meaning of poverty, where we hit a complete impasse. He said poverty only had merit if deliberately chosen out of love for God; I said many people had no choice in this matter and could merit by accepting it out of love for God. His rebuttal was based on the parable of the talents in which mere acceptance was not enough; somehow, a talent given had to be doubled in return. Since this was purely an economic perspective, I couldn't buy it.

At any rate, the story ends with my going to church as usual — but only after he had given me to ponder Pascal's Wager: what if? and just in case!

At school the next day I said nothing to my friends. Though I wondered why they stood on the sidelines and did not play, I didn't ask. As far as I was concerned, their case was closed; but thanks to them, my case as a Christian was now wide open.

Because of our on-going discussions, I soon realized my faith rested on an intellectual assent, and that the underpinnings of the Church itself were its rational foundations. I came to assume that any crack in this edifice and a man could be left dangling. For this reason I eventually found it more beneficial to study Greek philosophy than theology itself; in this way too, I could avoid thinking about Christ on any other than rational grounds — cold grounds, to be sure, but solid nonetheless. Still, in the back of my mind there ever lurked the possibility this might not be the whole story and that for me, at least, Christ could have an entirely different meaning. I continually put this notion aside, however, because if such a meaning existed, the door of my understanding was as closed as it was on the day the possibility first arose — that tragic day in church.

In the meantime, my father was taking a course in navigation in order to use his boat in the Coast Guard Auxiliary during the war. This course entailed a series of lectures at the Planetarium to which I went along as his eager companion and born star-gazer. The following year he took me to spend a weekend on Mount Wilson where we could see the reality of a sky no planetarium can project. Here I was overwhelmed — the stars, the mountains, and the reclusive life of the astronomer; this was it! Investigating the cosmos far from the problems of the world, this was where I belonged; this was my true vocation. To this end, I often attended the Saturday afternoon lectures at the Planetarium and by the time I was fifteen, never missed these pleasant afternoons. One such afternoon turned into a momentous occasion that marked the first of two major turning points in my life.

In the middle of Dr. Muellar's lecture there came the familiar leap, and immediately I felt caught between two loves. I held to my seat almost stubbornly until I realized God had not passed this time, but seemed to linger instead. The thought he might notice me, glance in my direction, was electrifying; after all, I had a lot of questions to ask. At the top of my list was the exact identification of this "leap" within, and its true relationship to God.

Though I had been taught that God was present in all things, the *experience* of this presence was somewhat of a problem, one I had been chasing down from the age of five. Whenever I questioned my father about these experiences, he would all but deny that man could experience God as He was in Himself. God was the cause, a special grace to be sure, but the effects were our own. As a child I believed him, and took my unusual experiences for some mysterious aspect of myself — alone. But over a period of time this conviction grew less convincing. By watching carefully, I discerned that my feelings, emotions, and certainly my thoughts, were quite separate and apart from something else that could leap and spread joy at some of the most inopportune moments. In itself it had a magnetic drawing-power which could not be ignored and, sometimes, not resisted. If I only knew for certain this was God, I felt it would change my life, because it would be the completion of a puzzle, the end of my search, and a key to the mystery of my life.

For this reason, when God seemed to linger a moment I quickly asked: what is this in me that recognizes you? The answer I received can be explained, but not demonstrated; it was more than an understanding or a certitude. It was a type of seeing I would only recognize as such later on. I simply saw a unique blending of the God without and the God within, the same identical cause, but a cause that gave rise to different manifestations which, in turn, gave rise to different experiences. It were as if each manifestation had its own accompanying experience. But however this worked, I now knew that *God who passed by was also the God that remained* and with this news I was jubilant. I wanted to shout "hooray!" and I might have said something aloud because the man next to me went "sh!"

Naturally I couldn't sit still with this. The lecture was now meaningless. I had to get outside and share this joy with my friends — the hills, the sky, and all the animals. Now I understood why I loved them so much and what they had been trying to tell me all along. We were the same, we were one — all of us, vessels of God!

I'm afraid I stepped on a lot of toes making my way to the exit of the darkened room. Once outside the lecture hall, I raced across the rotunda and out into the bright sunlight where I felt as if I had suddenly been struck blind, for the pain in my eyes was excruciating. I had to sit for a long time with my head in my hands before I could look squintingly out on the hillside. On doing so, I was disappointed at first because everything looked so much the same. But never mind, I now had the key to all this marvel, a marvel to which I too belonged. There was so much to think about, I decided that instead of taking the bus, I would walk the miles home; then too, I wanted to be out of doors to share this joy with my friends along the way.

Immediately following this insight, there came weeks of a terrible restlessness, which at first I could hardly formulate to myself. Something was still missing. After a while I discovered what it was, and felt it imperative to get one more answer from God. I had to find out where I, personally,

fit into this whole thing. God on the inside, God on the outside, but what about me? What was I worth to God? Was I
(and all nature included) merely a vessel, a disposable show-
case, here today and gone tomorrow? What, if any, is the
relationship of the vessel to its contents? The thought that
there was no permanent connection caused a terrible sense
of emptiness, as if I counted for absolutely nothing. To be
left out of Christ's plan had been tragic and outrageous, but
to be left out of this greater plan was so bewildering; the
very thought of it would leave me as energyless as if the bottom had fallen out of life. This awful sensation left no doubt
there was something wrong, there was something more I
needed to understand and, for the first time, I began to pray
in earnest. The answer to this question was crucial, more so
than any other I had asked for in my life — God must let me
have it!

Since I had little time to pray during the day, one evening I decided to pray all night. I don't remember how I
prayed, but I was always quite verbal with the petitions
which were more like arguments than prayers. I was also
generous with the vows and by this time had made so many,
I couldn't keep track of them, but they were becoming useless anyway. Beyond a certain point, there was no turning
back even if I had wanted to. Something in me was always
forging ahead; it was all I could do to keep up with it, and
right now, it threatened to go on without me.

I didn't have to pray long before the notion of the Trinity hit me like a bolt of lightning. There, at the beginning of
a line of light was the Father, the Creator, the God without;
and here, at the end of the line was the Holy Spirit, the leap
of joy, the God within; but midway in this path of light was
Christ. Instantly I wanted to know: what was Christ doing
in the Trinity? Though I had blessed myself a million times,
perhaps, I had never thought about him in this way. I began
going through my repertory of explanations: God-man, re-
deemer, mediator, exemplar. . . everything I could think of,

but none of them satisfying. His presence in the Trinity was something else again, and I couldn't put my finger on it. In the meantime, my original question had been forgotten; instead, I put my mind to work on this question of Christ's meaning in the Trinity, and how he fit into the great plan of God I was beginning to discover.

I stayed up thinking about this until I could stretch my mind no further and went to bed, but not to sleep. I tossed and turned until almost morning when, finally, I felt myself relaxing, beginning to drift...then the answer came and woke me up. Christ's position in the Trinity stood for everyman and his relationship to God. His humanity was the vessel, the meeting place where God within and without had fruition and became whole, so that everything created and uncreated was united and One. To know this same fruition as Christ had known it in himself, the vessel must become perfect as he was perfect. Christ was the medium through which the vessel (me) could become one with its content (God).

I never had to think about this for a minute; I knew exactly what to do next. I jumped out of bed, got dressed, and under the streetlights and early morning fog, walked to church to make my peace with Christ. Later I came home, gave away all my clothes and sold my books because now, I had to follow.

It didn't take long, however, to realize my struggles with Christ were not over, but were in some respects, just beginning. Before long I found myself in the company of those whose sentiments and devotions to the historic Christ had no precedence in myself. I had no head for images and was never granted a single experience of God in which the historic Christ was object. It was as if he refused to be an object to my mind and emotions however hard I tried, in the beginning, to make this possible. Instead, he was the medium turning my gaze, not upon himself, but upon the still-point within. At first this was disconcerting and, once again, I felt left out. The path of the saints has always had Christ as the object of its meditations, insights, visions, and experiences; in this I could find no exceptions. Yet, for myself, I could make none of these things happen; it was like trying to beat against a stone wall. I had to learn the hard way the futility of my own desires in this matter.

How then was I to identify with Christ in the reality of the here and now? Without a doubt, if it hadn't been for the Eucharist I would surely have lost track of Christ again. But in the Eucharist, Christ's presence was as invisible and formless as his grace and work in me. Thus it became my lifeline to the Trinity, drawing me into its silence and giving me the certitude that here I had finally come home; this was where I belonged, and accordingly, I took my place.

This then is how I came upon a middle way of traveling the contemplative life. Like a stream, I made my way between the high peaks of the rational on the one side, and the mystical peaks of extraordinary experience on the other. The stream did not climb upward, but ever coursed downward in search of its own level — its ultimate destiny in still waters. This is not a transcendent path because the stream stays low and clings to the earth, escaping none of the turbulence in the ordinary flow of life. Still, it's a dangerous course. Because the terrain is ever-changing, it is impossible to chart the path ahead of time and thus, without direction, I often had no idea where I was going or how it would all end. Sometimes I was carried along against my will, and even with fear, by a movement not of myself. Learning not to struggle against the current was, for ten years, my peculiar contemplative journey until one day, the stream disappeared and traveled underground for many miles and many years before once more emerging to see the light. Only this time, the light would cast no shadow because now there would be no object in its path.

While taking this first journey, I never forgot the tragic

eyes that followed me that day in church. I often pondered
the possibility they presented: that Christ's death might
have a significance other than those traditionally assigned to
it. But since this was only an intuition without a counterpart
in my understanding, I continually pushed it aside. That it
waited almost forty years for a resolution is something else
to ponder, yet it became a reality on this second journey —
the journey beyond the self — when the door of my understanding gave way to reveal a lost dimension of Christ, a dimension I would never have imagined possible.

In this present movement, Christ literally exploded in a
crisis that would efface him totally and, at the same time,
reveal him in a new and different way. One by one, the
Trinity vanished. First came the loss of self, the vessel, the
medium — Christ; next came the loss of God within, the
still-point — the Holy Spirit; and finally I lost the God without, the Father and great Oneness. But with each loss came
a compensating insight. With the loss of self, Christ dissolved into the still-point; they were One, and all that remained of this human experience. Suddenly, this too disappeared and all that remained was the One God seen everywhere. When this disappeared, there was only a terrible
void, and I came upon the death of God, a crucifixion unknown even by our psychological standards, since the state
of complete unknowing is hardly recognizable when there is
nothing known to which it can be compared.

I have called this great void and state of unknowing, a
Passageway. It was during this time, when doing my utmost
to acclimate or get used to this state, that a distant voice
broke through the silence. I had been walking on a secluded
road and stopped to look around at my old friends — the
hills, trees, and wild grasses, now so empty and void; it was
a look of complete unbelievability. How could I have been
so duped, hoodwinked — and all my life! It was impossible
. . . yet, it had to be — there was nothing there. Then, above

the trees, I heard a distant voice asking his father why he had abandoned him, and with that, the door of my understandng began to give way.

I had never associated the Dark Nights with Christ's death. I could never make that match, but here, I understood this man and knew exactly where he was at. Never in history has a holy man, saint, or sage of any religion gone out of this world with such a question on his lips, or ended his life on such a note. This was indeed the death of God and a sign of contradiction to the end. No-self is a meaningless state, but no-God is an incomprehensible condition, yet a condition with which I could now identify and understand completely.

That he too had come to this end, this nothingness beyond all we can possibly call a self, was strangely comforting. Here we were, companions in a great mistake, allies even in the void. I was glad I had gone as far as he had and did not blame him for bringing me to this end. I wanted to see the same truth he had seen, and if this was it — if there was no God — then this was the end of the road. There were no regrets.

Christ had expected a resurrection just as I had expected to "see," but obviously it hadn't happened. Instead of glory, we had seen nothing; nothing perhaps, but the futility of our lives and even the pointlessness of our deaths. Yet coming upon him unexpectedly in the Passageway, I knew a closer identity with him for having been mistaken than I had ever known during all the years I thought he had been right. Now I understood the real tragedy — his and my own. It was the tragedy of all those who had believed in him, but would never come this far and would never understand a thing like this.

I was glad his loved ones had seen him after his death, at least in their own minds and hearts; after all, life must go on whether there's any truth in it or not. Someone had to stretch the human limits to find out if there was any truth beyond the self, any life beyond this one, or any God beyond belief. Christ could do no more because there is no more a man can possibly do — and what man has done as much? What is more, he did it not only for himself, but that others would not be afraid when their time came to stretch these same human limits. Now I knew and understood how one could go this far, and because I entertained no hope of going beyond Christ's own ending, I turned to face the great reality — the reality of absolute nothingness.

Shortly after this turning point, or point of final acceptance, I did in fact "see." And when I finally saw "that" which remains when there is no self, I thought of Christ and how he too had seen "that" which remained — a seeing which *is* the resurrection itself. That he never truly relinquished his certitude of eventually seeing, no one knows for sure; I think he did, because certitude must eventually yield to seeing when God-as-object yields to God-as-subject. Spanning this gap between object and subject is a perilous transition; in fact, this gap may be the only real void man can experience in this life or after. For Christ, it might have been made in a split second — or better still, three days. For myself, it took almost four months.

The particular type of seeing I refer to as the resurrection is the seeing of God, not as object, but as pure subject. During his lifetime, and on the cross, Christ always referred to his Father as object — as the One who sent him, gave him power, whose work he did, and whose will he followed. At the same time, he referred to his Oneness and union with the Father without claiming the absolute identity of pure subjectivity; but then, it would have been useless to make this claim since no one would have understood it anyway. This knowledge is beyond the capability of our understanding because pure subjectivity must be seen directly, and even then, cannot be comprehended by the intellect. If Christ had this pure subjective seeing during his life, we would not be able to explain his references to God-as-object, nor why he had to be resurrected when he lived in a resurrected state already. Had there been nothing human about him, this would be explainable; but then his life and death would not have been a reality.

Christ had a divine self — not like the self we know — and though he knew God in a subjective way as being inseparable from himself, it was still God-as-object; analogous, perhaps, to the knowledge of our own union with the divine. His agony and death was the foregoing of his divine self, his union with God, a prospect which is more than giving up the self as we know it; it is the giving up of a self made one with God. In this way his life is parallel to our own, wherein our first movement is coming to this union in which God is still object and "other" than ourselves; and the second movement: the relinquishing of this union, and coming upon God as he is in himself — God as pure subject.

That Christ knew this second movement and entered the gap between object and subject — or state of unknowing — is truly the death of God, but only God-as-object, not God-as-subject. In many ways this state of unknowing is a descent into hell, a great void and the passageway to seeing — the resurrection. Evidently not even a divine self, or a self that is one with God, can avoid making this transition or entering the gap between object and subject.

Nevertheless, I do not regard the resurrection as the final step; to see and know is not enough. Greater than this is the ascension, or final dissolution into the fullness of God. With the dissolution of his human form — seemingly into thin air — Christ suddenly becomes everywhere: the God within and without, as well as all form in which the manifested and unmanifested have fruition and become One. Thus, even the seeing of the Trinitarian aspects of God is not the final step. The final step is where there is no Trinity at all, or when all aspects of God are seen as One and all that Is.

I am as convinced today as I was momentarily con-

vinced as a child, that the real tragedy of Christ's death is
that so few understand it. The general interpretation is that
Christ gave up his self so the rest of us would not have to do
so. He did it, so now the rest of us are free. That we should
have a liberated self when Christ had no self, makes no
sense. Self is not our true life or our real nature; it is but a
temporary mechanism, useful for a particular way of knowing, and in every way equivalent to our notion of original
sin. Self may not be sin, but certainly it is the cause of sin,
and what needs to be overcome is not the effects, but the
cause itself. To be forgiven is not enough; we must put an
end to the very need to be forgiven.

In this way, self is the sin to be overcome and when it
is overcome, then we are truly free. Christ did not overcome
our individual self for us; he only showed us by his death
what we too will have to go through to be free of sin, be it in
this life or after death. Christ not only mediates this overcoming of self, but is "that" which goes beyond the self to
endure the passage and finally see.

As emphasized before, the bewildering aspect of this
journey was the failure to recognize "that" which remained
when there was no self. The stillness and emptiness within
was just that and nothing more; no one, nothing, appeared
to take its place. Continually I was expecting the divine to
reveal itself within, but it never happened; obviously the
final seeing was not to be of this nature. Here I think of how
Christ's loved ones also failed to recognize him after his resurrection, because without a self, Christ cannot be recognized in this fashion any longer. Thus, he had to reveal himself to them all over again in a totally new and different
light. It is in this light that the subjectivity of God is known
and can only be known. It is not the light of belief, but the
light of disbelief, since what is seen ever remains unbelievable to the thinking mind. To say that "God is all that is" is
not only unthinkable and unbelievable, but to some, it is
absolute blasphemy. Our minds cannot comprehend this; it

must be seen to be believed and yet, once it is *seen*, it is no longer believed. In this way then, our belief or frame of reference eventually gives way to seeing.

If I had never had a self, I would not be able to understand why man clings so tenaciously to the certitude of its permanence. Whoever was responsible for dividing the self into lower and higher parts (of man) commmitted a serious crime against humanity. This division has given rise to the notion that the lower (ego and immature) self must be overcome while the higher (fully integrated) self must be sought as the goal of human realization. Out of ignorance, I too clung to this system of belief because I had been led to believe it was this higher self that would be united with God, here and for all eternity. It took a long time before my experiences led me to doubt this conviction and, at the same time, let in the possibility that this was not the whole truth.

It was in moments before the journey when, overcome by what lies beyond the self, I learned something was yet wanting; there was still another step — this was not the end. I intuited a far greater and more final surrender that made me afraid at times; but the day this fear disappeared was the day self disappeared and the journey began. Before this happens, however, I am convinced one's trust in God, the great Unknown, must be tried in fire; otherwise this fear remains and will never be overcome. The final relinquishing of self (the higher self) may therefore constitute the only true act of faith in God a man can make; clinging to God, our union, and experiences of Him, may be a great mistrust and the ultimate expression of disbelief.

At one time I believed self was necessary in order to love God — if I didn't (or we didn't), who would? This was the reason of our birth and the meaning of our lives: to love God. But shortly before this journey, I discovered that self does not love God at all, because "that" which loves God in ourselves is God himself. To say it is "I" who loves, is to unwittingly deflect selfward and claim for the self what belongs to God alone. Only God is love, and for this love to fully realize itself, self must step aside. And not only do we not need a self to love God, but for the same reason, we do not need a mind to know him; that in us which knows God, is God himself.

Before crossing over the line to the Unknown — and becoming unknown myself — I had been given to understand that from now on, it would be God loving Himself not *in* me, but *in* Himself. I found this confusing and wrote pages on the issue. I was already convinced it was not I who loved, because the love I experienced was beyond the self already; rather, it was Christ in me who loved the father — or God loving himself — but still, it was in *me*. Perhaps it was the Holy Spirit loving the Father in Christ and not in me...I finally gave up on this enigma saying, I do not fully understand, and let it go at that. Two years and an unusual journey later, I did understand. It meant that God would no longer be loved as an object (in me) but as pure subject (in Himself), but how this works must be seen, because it cannot be adequately communicated or even experienced.

It is one step, and a giant one, to see clearly and participate in the love that flows between the persons of the Trinity, but here too, God is seen as the object of his own love. It is yet another step to realize that God is One absolute Subject and is Himself love-without-an-object. One God, one love, nothing else exists. This then is the step beyond our highest experiences of love and union, a step in which self is not around to divide, separate, objectify, or claim anything for itself. Self does not know God; it cannot love him, and from beginning to end has never done so. Anyone who has experienced this love surely realizes that it is beyond any and all capacity of a self. If it were not, there would be no going out of self — no overcoming of sin.

After this account had been written, there occurred what I call a "last experience," which resulted in an insight into the nature of Christ. I called it that because of its similarity to the very first experience I had, at the age of five, and its recurrence at this time gave a sense of closure to my life, the quest of forty-five years. Before recounting this insight, however, I will first describe the two experiences themselves.

The earlier experience came as an overwhelming surprise. I had been on my way to play a game of cops-and-robbers with my friends when I felt a swift, powerful welling up inside me that stopped me in my tracks. From within I seemed to be expanding in all directions though I could see no visible signs of this and had no idea what it was. Yet I knew it to be so awesome and overpowering it could not be contained and, for a moment, I thought it might squeeze me out and take over. I was frightened and thought to myself: I'm gonna bust! But at what seemed to be the peak of its expansion, it stopped; I held my breath in suspense, then across my mind came the words "you're too big for yourself!" and with that, came an explosion of wild joy like the sound of a great voice laughing. After this it gradually disappeared and all was as usual — though I was never to be the same again.

I did not think of this as an experience of God; at the same time, I was certain it was not myself. But from that day forward I could see this mysterious power within, which became an ever-present friends and teacher. After four years it vanished, however, and was not seen again until I came upon God in the woods. The relentless quest of tracking down the true nature of this experience was the search of a lifetime; and it is because of its similarity to this first experience that I call the following, a "last experience." I take it from my journal.

What I saw take place was just a possibility, which I experienced only briefly. It was almost frightening. I saw how God can invade a form, take over a human form. This is perhaps the most total loss of self possible. In this invasion there is power unimaginable, and the only consciousness remaining says "I am God." There is something almost frightening about this type of total possession. I saw how I do indeed have something left of my own. After all, my words and actions are my own and I am always aware that I am not the totality of God, and that there is something left that could be done here. This was not an explosion outwards but an invasion inwards, a possession like the swift blowing up of a balloon, like the act of creation; only here, the form was already waiting. I don't know what to make of this but I am skeptical. I do not know what It may do in this form — just how human is this divine life? All this reminds me of Christ; this must have been his own experience. I see how this would be so — see it clearly. Yes, he is one with God and is God himself — as much as is humanly possible. At the same time, though possessed and full of God, Christ is not the totality of God because a man's form and faculties limit God and yet, somehow they don't. God is not limited by form; the form is merely the act of THAT which never changes and ever remains unknowable. But the act, the form, is knowable and limited not by God, but my our own uncomprehending minds.

I saw how this possession or invasion works. It can be frightening. To lose yourself is one thing; to become God is another. I think I would just as soon stay in my present state, neither totally possessed nor totally myself. It is difficult to point out the difference between WHAT remains (when there is no self) and total possession; both are God yet one is full of God and neither has a self. In those moments of being possessed, I felt a bit of a struggle as if not sure, not understanding. It was all very risky and yet I knew there wasn't a thing I could do about it. I had no choice. So what does all this mean? I don't know, but what I do know for sure is that God can possess this form far more than He does at present. He can take over and obliterate any other consciousness but the one that says "I am God." I

don't know what to make of this but it's all very interesting. Maybe it's a foretaste of some future event. I
hope not!

Later I wrote at length about this incident and concluded that for God to infuse himself into me was like trying
to blow up a balloon with a thousand pinholes. Without a
self, form is porous. Here there is no self to capture or hold
onto the divine, no self for it to overshadow, work through,
or impose itself upon; nothing to which the divine could become attached. Thus, to have a divine mission, man needs a
self — a will, a driving energy, and above all, self-consciousness; therefore, Christ had to have a self to do God's
work on earth. But how did he come by this self? At one
time was his human self overlaid by the divine in a type of
union that has enabled men to become emissaries of God —
such as saints, seers, and prophets? God has always had
such mediums, so in what way was Christ different? In my
opinion, God's possession or infusion in Christ was more
than a union of the human and divine, more than that of a
man suddenly seized and overpowered by God.

Although no-self cannot be a medium, it nevertheless
stands in a unique position for such an actuality. In the absence of self, in a completely empty form unconditioned by
this world and untouched by self (sin) from the beginning,
God could create and fashion a type of self unknown by our
relative standards, even our highest standards of union with
God. Such an admixture of the human and divine is not only
incomprehensible, but it would be impossible of realization
at any stage of our self-becoming or union with God. No
matter how fervently we aspire for union with the divine we
cannot become other Christs, much less regard this as the
culmination of our own selfhood — God forbid! We cannot
identify our self and its type of consciousness with the self
God had fashioned in Christ. This means that if there is any
time in life we can honestly identify with Christ it is from

the position of no-self, or when we have entered the gap between object and subject.

Here we can truly identify with this man on the cross who willingly gave up his self, his powers, his union with God, to show us that God lies beyond not only our petty, secular notion of self, but our most divine notions as well. Until there is no self, I do not see how it is possible to have any true identity with Christ, because this ultimate identity, or no-self, is necessary if we are ever to "see." Until this point is reached, God remains an object — a power above, a love within, or however we care to envision God as being "other" than the self. And indeed, God *is* other than the self — on the cross he is no-self. For me at least, this is the true message and meaning of Christ where, even more than his words, he showed us by his death what each of us will have to go through to see — to be resurrected — to be free, free of sin which is the self.

In conclusion then, the incompleteness of my understanding of Christ, which began as a child, was the on-going struggle of my Christian life. Without this continual search for an honest level of identification with Christ, I would not have been Christian. What may be given to others at once was, for me, a slow revelation of painful honesty, continual questioning, and a determined struggle every step of the way.

It was a way of darkness and unknowing, so little understood by others that I was left to forge a way and go it alone. How could I identify with Christ when I could not use my imagination? had no experience of God in which he was the object? and more often than not, found the Gospels trite from sheer repetition? Evidently his mission in my life was not to be one of fulfilling emotional or intellectual needs; rather, it was that of a mediator who never permitted himself to be an object, but diverted my gaze to the still-point instead.

I could never equate the historic Christ with the still-point and yet, the notion that he lived in some remote heaven was equally unacceptable. I could not identify with his selfhood because I knew it to be of a totally different nature than my own. Much less could I identify with Christ on a symbolic level because from earliest childhood, I have never believed in fairy-tales — once removed as they are from reality and truth. Christ is not a symbol of anything, but is the great reality himself, and to find this reality was the quest — my life's work.

I looked upon his historical life as over. The message remained, the grace was always there, but the man was gone. With his ascension into heaven I felt he had dissolved into the fullness of God, so that the continual effort to separate him out — be it on an imaginative, emotional, or intellectual level — was on my part, worse than dishonest; it was a phoniness I could not live with. So how then could I identify with this incomprehensible man-God, and identify with him in truth, in the here and now?

Gradually I figured out a way. His presence in the Eucharist was mystical, his grace was mystical, and his work in me was mystical — a work done in silence and darkness. Thus, to accept him on these, his own terms, I had to meet him on the same level: a mystical level that for me, was deep, hidden, unknown, and inexpressible. Here I could identify with Christ as he gradually imparted to me his own vision of the kingdom of God — the still-point within. Because of this, it could easily be said that I never knew Christ personally — on the level of personalities, that is — and on this level, he did in fact elude me all my life. Nevertheless at the end of the present journey, I finally confronted this man in a smile-of-recognition. And with this smile, my understanding was complete, the struggle was over.

Christ is not the self, but that which remains when there is no self. He is the form (the vessel) that is identical with the substance — and he is not one form, but all form. Christ is the act, the manifestation and extension of God that is not separate from God. We cannot comprehend "that" which acts or "that" which smiles, but we all know the act — the smile that is Christ himself. Thus, Christ turns out to be all that is knowable about God, because without his acts, God could not be known. Act itself is God's revelation and this revelation is not separate from God, but *is* God himself. This I believe, is what Christ would have us see; this is his completed message to man. But who can understand it?

Complete understanding can only come at the end of the journey because full, complete understanding from the beginning would nullify any necessity of taking a journey. For me at least, this was my life, my Christian life, with its on-going struggle for an honest, absolutely truthful, final identification with Christ. Belief and understanding are only complete once we see, but once we see "what" Christ is then we can answer "where" Christ is, because these cannot be separated. Once we see the absolute subjectivity of God, then we can answer the question "Where is Christ?" Christ is everywhere. He is all that Is — all, of course, but the self.

Pure Subjectivity

Not long ago, I had the good fortune to discuss this account with a contemplative priest who is also an experienced spiritual director and scholar in the varied traditions of the Christian contemplative life. From the outset he made it clear he could not concede the non-existence of the self at any stage because, from beginning to end, life is a series of subject-object or I-Thou relationships. Subjective union with an objective God annihilates neither subject nor object, nor does it discontinue their relationship; if this were so, who could affirm this union? Who could return from a transient experience of loss-of-self to declare he had no self? To say there is no self may be one way to describe such an experience, but it is not the way to establish such a reality which, in his opinion, could not be done. What is more, he found the circumstances of discussing no-self somewhat humorous. Here we were, he pointed out, two distinct individuals and personalities with two disagreeing minds, discussing our relationship with God. What could be more obvious or self-evident than these relationships? How could we ever get away from them? And if we could, what would be left to discuss?

Needless to say, I was fully aware of the problems involved in any discussion of no-self. I had already learned how empirical reality stands in the way as a barrier, not only limiting our vision, but limiting any discussion of no-self as well. Seemingly this barrier is the failure to realize that the reality we see, hear, feel, and think is so perishable, we can grind it down to a few elementary particles that even then, continue to baffle the mind. Nevertheless, I do not regard empirical reality as a true barrier to vision; on the contrary, it is the gateway through which we must pass in order to see what, if anything, lies on the other side. But the irony of this passage is that empirical reality is not seen as a barrier until the other side is reached, at which time, it is seen as no barrier at all. Therefore, it is only in retrospect we see this as a barrier to *others*, while knowing it is also the gate through which all must pass. Because I was aware of this, I readily understood my friend's point of view — at one time, my sole point of view — and realizing he did not share my present perspective, knew we were in agreement nevertheless, when using the same empirical data, the same tools as a common ground for discussion. It was like standing in a gateway discussing how far ahead we could see — an agreeable position, I felt, from which to disagree.

Those in a less advantageous position would be those who have skirted or surmounted empirical reality by some intellectual endeavor, without passing through it experientially. This could lead to a denial of empirical reality and, by making the ground we walk on a mere illusion, pull the rug out from under any meaningful discussion. When we cannot discuss what lies two feet ahead because it would be too un-understandable or too ineffable to do so, the subjects that matter most in life become so esoteric and privileged, they end up belonging to a few superior men; as someone once said to me, "when you see the world as illusion, you will have become a superman." Even if this incentive had not come too late, I would have preferred to pass through the gate of the known and remain as is, which means to discuss what is when the chance arises, as it did on this occasion.

What I discovered in the course of our discussion was how pure subjectivity was the keystone on which the ex-

perience of self either rises or falls. Though we didn't discuss
the subject directly, it became clear that the possibility of
passing from an ordinary subjective condition (or subject-
object type of consciousness) to a condition of pure subjectivity (in which subject and object are identical) was the major clue to the disappearance of the self. The possibility of
making this transition between two opposing types of consciousness or two different ways-of-knowing is important,
because if this transition is *not* possible, self remains; but if
the transition *is* possible, then self does not remain. The
reason for saying this, I will attempt to put forward since it
is the subject and concern of everything that follows.

Before proceeding, however, I must admit to being
prejudiced in the matter. After making this journey, I have
no choice but to believe this transition can not only be
made, but that it is inherent in everyone to do so whether
they realize it or not. Though I do not understand how it
can be made on a purely intellectual or technical level, I am
nevertheless familiar with the experiential aspects of such a
crossing; so if the following explanation appears clumsy, it
is because the particular level or view from which I speak
does not always allow for logical fulfillment.

I will begin with my own definition of pure subjectivity. Basically, it is a way of knowing in which the knower,
the known, and the knowing, are identical and inseparable.
This identity, however, is not the identity of empirical or
visual form; it is not the identity of mind or content or of
anything generally falling within the realm of the known.
Rather, it is the identity of a subject and object unknowable
to the mind, an identity known only to itself. The basic
knowledge of this identity is that it exists and knows itself as
all that exists; thus, pure subjectivity is the eye of seeing itself, and wherever it looks it sees nothing but itself. It
knows no within or without, nor would it be proper to ask
"who" or "what" this eye belongs to, because any answer
would give rise to a division between knower and known,

which is not how this identity works. The eye seeing itself knows no "I, me, or mine" since it knows nothing that is not "I, me, or mine" and therefore has no need to make such a distinction. It does not *belong* to an individual subject or self, nor does it inhere in any thing or any object, because it *is* everything and belongs only to itself. In pure subjectivity there is no separation of the I and Thou or this and that because these words are mere labels for an empirical reality that falls short of the whole truth when it fails to unveil the eye seeing itself. Yet, despite the problem inherent in the use of words, I call this eye seeing itself "pure subjectivity" because it is the one subject, the one existent, in which there is complete identity between its existence, its knowing and its doing.

But there is another way of knowing that does not belong to the eye seeing itself. This is a condition of consciousness in which the knower is not identical with the known and thus, the subject always remains separate and divided from its object. This is our ordinary type of subjectivity in which everything known, including the self, is an object of consciousness, and this type of knowing (or consciousness) never sees itself directly, because as soon as it looks at itself, it sees itself as an object, not as a subject. For this reason, the subject can only be known through an objective method, made possible by a reflexive mechanism of the mind bending back on itself, whereby the subject can be aware of its own awareness, its own feelings and thoughts. Because of this objectifying mechanism, we know ourselves as subjects; and to know ourselves as subject by any other method is virtually impossible.

It seems that some people would have us believe that even when we do not reflect back on ourselves or see ourselves as objects we are, nevertheless, still aware of ourselves as subjects; but based on my experiences, this is not the way it works. Instead, I discovered that when you can no longer see yourself as object, you soon lose the ability to be aware of yourself as subject. This, at least, was my finding, and I think a simple test can reveal how this works.

Let us say, for the moment, it was possible for the subject to see itself as the subjective eye turned upon itself — what would it see? Obviously it would see absolutely nothing; if it saw "something," this something would only be an object to consciousness and would not be the subject to consciousness. This means that when we come upon the true subject of consciousness, we come upon nothing at all. We could not say the self-as-subject is identical with the self-as-object since nothing cannot be identical with something. It also means that self-as-object is not the true subject to consciousness because the true subject is unknowable — it is nothing to the mind.

From this we can conclude that all we know about ourselves (or self-as-object) is not only secondhand knowledge, it is not even the truth! Here the age-old dictum "know thyself" turns out to be the impossible dream. Like the myth of finding a pot of gold at the end of the rainbow, we dig and dig only to discover there is nothing there.

It is quite possible that at some time or other everyone has made contact with the self-as-subject. All that is required for such an encounter is the cessation of the reflexive movement of the mind bending back on itself. Without this reflexive (or pre-reflexive) movement, we are no longer aware of our own awareness, our own feelings and thoughts, and thus we have encountered self-as-subject. But since this subjective self is as nothing to the mind, we cannot stay in this condition for long and soon fall back into self-consciousness or self-as-object. To remain in this unreflexive condition for any length of time would mean encountering an emptiness, a void, a nothingness that *is* the subjective self — which I have called no-self.

As a contemplative, I was familiar with this condition and ever found it quiet, dark, and restful; sometimes it was even the gateway to "that" which lies beyond no-self. Yet it never occurred to me that this non-reflexive condition of the mind could become a permanent state. I could not see the possibility of remaining in this state while carrying out the ordinary mental and physical activities of daily life; thus, even if I had heard of such a possibility, I would not have deemed it a desirable or feasible way of practical living. Furthermore, I never believed in deliberately manipulating the mind because my particular contemplative path took the way of least resistance: by waiting effortlessly for some form of divine intervention. As I conceived it, spending my whole life waiting for God *was* the good life.

Whether or not there honestly exist certain techniques of mind-manipulation that can bypass the need for divine intervention, or the need to wait upon God, is something I do not know. Nor can I imagine how anyone can put a permanent, irrevocable end to the reflexive movement of the mind without running into certain psychological dangers. The danger would lie in not knowing how to proceed once this mechanism had been overcome or closed down. Without some compensating or sustaining factor arriving on the scene, the state of no-self is no guarantee of ecstasy or bliss, because once the relatively peaceful effects have worn off, no-self can become — as I discovered in the Passageway — a very burdensome, if not a dire state of affairs.

But if I do not know how this reflexive mechanism of the mind can come to an end by any effort of our own, I do know it can happen, because it happened to me. The journey began with the inability of the mind to make self an object, or when the ability to be self-conscious was no longer possible. The reflexive mechanism had ceased to function and thereafter left a subtle, almost physical feeling that some aspect of my mind was being "held." Whether this aspect was (and is now) being held back, held up, held down, or just held in a steady gaze upon the Unknown, I do not know. But whatever its reality, I know that the ability to make self an object was forever altered, cut off, or made immovable. Unknown to myself, at the time, the day this happened was the day the first step in a transition from ordinary consciousness to pure subjectivity had been made.

Before this event took place, I had never noticed how automatically and unconsciously the mind was aware of itself, or how continually conscious I had been of my own awareness in all mental processes, or in all my thoughts, words, and deeds. But when this reflexive movement came to an end, I suddenly realized the profound roots of self-consciousness, roots that unknowingly had infiltrated every aspect of my existence. To have this entire system uprooted, made for so many amazing discoveries as I moved through the ordinary affairs of life that I could never hope to recount them all. It would have been impossible to make these discoveries all at once, or to anticipate them in advance, because it was only when meeting with each of the many facets of living that I realized how new and different life had become. It took the most ordinary events and encounters to gradually bring this new life into focus and thus, enable me to become aware of the full extent of this alteration. During the journey, I called this gradual process of learning, the process of acclimation.

Having made this first step in the transition, it might be thought I was overwhelmed by the nothingness of no-self, but fortunately this was not the case. Initially I could give no thought to my own emptiness when I felt I had entered the mysterious flow of a greater life, wherein the experience of self and no-self were equally unimportant issues.

Furthermore, I discovered that when consciousness of the self is removed, "pure objectivity" seems to take over; without the ability to look inward anymore, I looked outward upon empirical objects to see in them what I had never seen before. What I saw was how particular, singular, and individual objects dissolved into a great Unknown, an Unknown that was the same throughout all empirical variety and multiplicity.

The only object that did not give way or reveal the unknown was the subject to this objective consciousness; for although the physical, empirical subject (personality) remained unchanged, there could not be found therein any true subject of consciousness — any seer of the Oneness into which all other objects emptied and became lost to the mind. Whatever observed this Oneness was not known to be identical with it, nor could it be localized anywhere within the empirical form; instead, that which saw this Oneness seemed to be above my forehead and outside anything I could call a self. Thus, the self I once knew was gone; and the self I never knew? Well, it would be difficult to miss something I never knew; but somewhere between the two, there remained the silence and stillness of no-self.

Although the known self had disappeared, an outsider might insist that logically, the self as the unknown subject remains. But if the only reason we can give for the existence of an unknown subject is the fact it is a logical and intellectual necessity, then our reasoning stands on shaky ground indeed. When a logical entity cannot be backed by a knowable, functional reality, the self-as-subject makes as much sense as the insistence that a man who has lost an arm, retains it. If the self cannot be seen, known, felt, or used, then what good is it? As a noun or pronoun "self" is a helpful word in an empirical world, but when used to designate anything absolute or permanent, the notion of self is not only unhelpful, it could be deceptive, and clinging to its purely logical existence, the great illusion of all time.

Here on the first step of the transition, the "logical subject" has evidently given way to a state of consciousness in which there is no known subject, and the one real object of consciousness remaining is the Oneness of all that exists. While this step ushers in a new way of knowing, it is not the way of knowing characteristic of pure subjectivity; to come upon this final seeing, two more steps are necessary. Before proceeding to these steps, however, I would like to attest to the great sense of wonder and beauty made possible by this first phase of the transition. To be free of the self and thereby enter the greater flow of life, means to see the Oneness of existence, its sacredness, and deathlessness, as well as this world's dynamic link with God in which all life is virtually an aspect of Himself. I often wondered why this state of affairs could not last forever, but I now see this was not the final step; it was only the first step into a new existence and a whole new way of knowing. It was just a beginning.

The second step (lasting about four months) was by far the most difficult period of my life, and of my own accord it was a step I would never have taken, not for all the promises in heaven. Though I cannot account for the exact mechanism that brings it about, it makes sense to say that without a knowable subject, we must soon be without a knowable object, since subject and object are functionally relational and not just logically so. Sooner or later the relation between a knowable object and an unknowable subject must fall apart when no relationship can possibly be established. At the same time, it appears as if the emptiness of the empirical subject had finally caught up with, and engulfed, all empirical objects in its own nothingness. Thus, in the absence of a subject, the initial compensating factor of pure objectivity eventually gave way to reveal the absolute void of all objects to the mind.

This second step seems to be a state of consciousness in which there is neither subject nor object, and if any relationship persists between knower and known, it is the identity of absolute nothingness. This is a state of complete unknowing, wherein the usual methods of knowing have been cut off, and the only knowable thing remaining is an empty, meaningless, empirical reality. What is more, while in this state, there were times when I doubted if even consciousness remained because it too, had a curious way of disappearing and leaving nothing in its wake.

When this happened, or when ordinary consciousness

gave way, the result was not unconsciousness — which I would have regarded as a blessing — rather, the remaining factor was the most rudimentary source of life I had ever come upon. It was an unknowable (unexperiential) life that seemed to remain unaffected and outside anything we ordinarily regard as life or consciousness. At seeing this, I felt I had never sunk so low, because it only brought home the fact that all my usual notions and experiences regarding life, death, and consciousness, had no reality whatsoever. "This" that lay below the level of consciousness, this was true life. Had I been empirically dead, coming upon eternal life might have been a marvelous occasion, but as it stood, the situation was impossible; I could neither come nor go. But of one thing I was sure: this life was not my own.

Since there was no way out of this bind or state of unknowing, all I could do was stay with the ordinary empirical affairs of life which, out of necessity, was not hard to do since most of life is lived on this level anyway. I had been so conditioned that living normally, with little or no thought, was easily done, and for this I was most grateful. It was here I reaped the benefit of the years of preparation prior to taking the journey. Although they were years when I often felt nothing was happening, I was now grateful for the most ordinary activity and routine cares that filled my life because they enabled me to keep going and to maintain a steady keel in a most difficult time.

Though empty and meaningless, empirical reality was all that was left. It was the one sure thing there was, and for all I knew, it was all that remained in the absence of both a subject and object to consciousness. I should add here that it is a mistake to think that the sheer materiality of objects constitutes a valid object of consciousness. In this stage I learned the difference between mere conditioning that enables us to get around in our environment without accident or stress, and true objects to consciousness that have value, meaning, and depth of relationship; it was this latter content which was now a complete void to my mind.

Though all doors to knowing had been tightly closed, there remained nevertheless a way out — a way I would not have dreamt possible. Without any means of knowing what remains in the absence of subject and object, the burden of proof falls squarely on whatever it *is* that does remain, which means it can make itself known — it can reveal itself. There may be no guarantee this will happen, but I believe no one sets out on such a journey unless this revelation has been intended from the beginning. And it is this timely revelation that brings about the third and final step in the transition between two incompatible ways of knowing.

Evidently the revelation of what remains, knows its own time and will only appear when it cannot possibly be mistaken for something else, or when the ground has been so thoroughly prepared, no weeds can grow up to choke its truth or ever hide it again. Once the ground is cleared of all obstacles or objects of consciousness, that which remains comes in the dark like a single shaft of light casting no shadows — no doubt or error — and thus, it is seen as nothing ever seen before.

For me, this disclosure occurred in the simple empirical gesture of a smile whereby *the smile itself, that which smiled, and that at which it smiled were known as identical.* In the immediacy of this way of knowing, the three aspects of the One were clear. Yet, Oneness predominates because the eye, to see and know itself, looks neither within nor without — as if having a subject and object — nor does it look at anyone or any thing; indeed, it does not "look" at all. It has not revealed itself to another. Rather, its revelation might be compared to the first manifestation of physical reality: when spirit, lying below the threshold of the known, first rose to the level of matter. When this occurred, there was no one around to witness or applaud such a feat, only the eye itself was present to rejoice in its own act, its own being, its own manifestation — thus, it revealed itself to no one and to no thing.

I should add that it would be incorrect to compare this revelation to some newly discovered content suddenly rising from an unconscious to a conscious level. The eye seeing itself lies outside and beyond all conscious and unconscious content, which is why every notion and every last fragment of content had first to be cleared away before its identity could be revealed. In fact, the eye is not consciousness; what it is, I do not know, but *that* it is — that I know. And because it exists and knows itself as all that is, I call it pure subjectivity and not pure consciousness. It is only because the eye seeing itself is also a way of knowing that it is analogous to our notion of consciousness, but apart from this, it is a mistake to equate the two.

The reason pure subjectivity is so difficult to communicate is that any description or interpretation must be done on a subject-object, or relative, level of understanding, which is inadequate for this task. To be understood properly, it must be known in the immediacy of its own identity, since it cannot be understood as being either a subject or an object of the mind. I would also add: as long as the mind can even reflect on the eye seeing itself, so long will it be unable to see it.

Certainly my own descriptions have fallen short when speaking of pure subjectivity in terms of ordinary consciousness. But I have only done so because pure subjectivity, like ordinary consciousness, has both a subject and an object, even though by relative standards, its subject and object remain unknowable. The subject is not the self or the I, the object is not the other or the non-I; rather, the subject and object are two identical aspects of the One eye, which is not transcendent in itself, but only transcendent to our ordinary consciousness. Yet, behind the closed door of our understanding, pure subjectivity is actually the way by which everything in existence knows itself; lying below or behind all levels and forms of consciousness, it is *that* which knows itself as all that exists.

Another reason why pure subjectivity defies adequate

description is that every account must be continually changing since the eye is not static; rather, it appears to open onto infinite possibilities in a movement of revelation that seemingly has no end. This movement is similar, perhaps, to our first glimpse of a forest that is revealed more fully as we approach its interior; so too, the eye expands, becomes more pervasive, and at the same time more concentrated and intense, as if drawing everything back into itself, into its own center.

How physical form can maintain itself against — or despite — the intensity of this movement, is a mystery, since form is ever on the brink of a glorious collapse. I find the mechanism for keeping everything from falling back into itself more awesome than even the outward thrust of creation. Though the movement of integration and disintegration (life and death) seems relatively slow, it is happening I think much faster than the mind can comprehend, for there seems to be no such thing as static maintenance.

Obviously, pure subjectivity is far more than a way of knowing, but what more this is, I do not know. Just coming upon it was the beginning of a new way of seeing and knowing for which the journey had been a necessary preparation. It's a simple kind of knowing, a type of knowledge-by-identity that is not extraordinary if we realize everything in the universe knows itself in this way, so why not man? That Christ came to save man — not the birds — from his "self" attests to our human deficiency in this matter. The cause of this deficiency is clear when we consider that of all we know to exist, only man has a self; only man feels lost because he cannot see. For this reason I tend to the view that man is on the bottom of the evolutionary heap (if such even exists), but I also see that his complexities have placed him in a unique position for a divine dispensation — as if God's own experiment had run amuck — and that despite his self, or possibly because of it, man will ultimately win out. But then, there is really no other way to go.

O

Recently, a friend told me that he could not stand the idea of God as pure subjectivity, because he found that people who believed this often became pompous frauds who paraded as God and went about seeking worshippers. I told him such behaviors could only arise from the failure to distinguish between the subjectivity of the self and the pure subjectivity of God. Anyone who says "I am God" could not have learned this distinction, because in the learning, the "I am" disappears and only "God" remains. Pure subjectivity is not the identity of self and God, but the identity of God alone who remains when there is no self. However, my friend assured me this was not the case. He said, those who claim to be God identify the subjectivity of the self with the subjectivity of God with no distinction in consciousness or way of knowing.

Since I did not encounter anything in this transition that could be called a self, I would be at a loss to explain how an identity between self and God (or self *as* God) could come about, or how a claim to personal deity could be made. I do not even hear Christ making such statements as "I am God." Always, he said everything came from the Father and not from his self.

For his part, my friend dismissed these claims of deification as belonging to the deranged mind, the religiously inflated ego, but offhand I could not do this. Instead, I feel open in these matters because I would very much like to know where, in this transition, it would have been possible to meet up with the self. For the moment, in the absence of an explanation, I can only conclude that no two people make the same journey, go through the same transition, or have the same experiences, even though in the end, the truth must be the same for all since the truth is not dependent upon anything but itself.

One suggestion, however, to help explain a claim for personal deification, would be that of mistaken identity, wherein the claimant, through some preconceived idea, understands his experience of God as the experience of his true self — or conversely, takes his self for God. It should be kept in mind that the variety of contemplative and religious experiences are so difficult to express and convey, there may be a tendency for the individual to plug his experiences into a ready-made frame of reference — an acceptable reference taken from those who have gone before. Thus, by inference or preconceived notion, pure subjectivity could be mistaken for the self when, in fact, the finding of the true self belongs to an entirely different journey.

Once again I would emphasize that the contemplative life is composed of two separate and entirely different movements: one of integration or the finding of the self; and one of disintegration or the losing of the self. In a religious context this would be, the movement toward union with God-as-object, followed by the second movement toward identity or God-as-subject. Of the two movements, it is far more likely that the movement toward union would culminate in experiences of personal deification, because further on, the experience of personal selfhood — on which personal deification depends — falls away. It is this very experience of no personal self and no personal God that composes the second movement. Thus, it does away with any possibility of a mistaken identity, especially when everything we thought we knew is taken away in a state of complete unknowing. Indeed, I find it difficult to see how anyone could emerge from this Passageway with any notions or preconceived ideas left intact!

What is more, the state of unknowing outlasts the Passageway and is, itself, the new way of knowing that never reverts back to the old way, for its displacement has been permanent and irreversible. There is no shifting back and forth between a relative and a non-relative way of knowing since the latter includes everything we ever need to know.

By the time the journey is over, the only possible way of living is in the now-moment, wherein the mind moves neither backward nor forward but remains fixed and fully concentrated in the present. Because of this, the mind is so open and clear that no preconceived notions can get a foothold; no idea can be carried over from one moment to another; much less, could any notion demand conformity from others. There are no more head-trips — no clinging to a frame of reference, even if it is only the reference of tomorrow's expectations. In a word, what is to be done or thought is always underfoot, with no need to step aside in order to find out what is to be thought, believed, or enacted.

In the now-moment the self never arises; nothing calls upon it do so. The eye seeing itself lives and holds everything tightly in this moment, a moment that has no need of a self. But even if we persist with the notion of self, such a label adds nothing to pure subjectivity. It tells us nothing more about it, and any clinging to self as a notion or an experience, certainly constitutes an obstacle to clear vision.

After stating these objections to my friend's notion of pure subjectivity — which I felt he had incorrectly understood — I asked him whether or not those who claim to be God, claim to be a part of the whole or the Whole itself? In his mood of humorous disgust for the entire notion, he went to dramatic lengths to assure me these drops of water claimed to be the whole of the sea, but could neither explain how the notion was derived, nor what experiences had given rise to such an assertion.

Here, I offered him my own understanding of the wholeness of God by comparing it to the drawing of a star, wherein the single points or extensions are its individual manifestations, but not its totality. For an individual manifestation to declare itself the star might be the partial truth, but not the whole truth. As the totality of *all* form, God is better visualized perhaps when the center of the star ex-

pands outward or retracts inward to form a single circle.
Either way, however, I do not see how a single manifestation that has been dissolved (retracted or expanded) into the
fullness of God can maintain itself in this human mode of
existence. My own experiences tell me this cannot be done
because there comes a point of no return, which is a point
when the present form of life can no longer maintain itself
against the tremendous, overwhelming force pulling back
into itself.

The disintegration of personal selfhood is just the beginning of this dissolution — this homeward journey — and
there is no point along the route at which anyone could say
"now I am God" — it would make no sense. At the same
time, there is no point at which we are not part of God, and
it is *this* point which is clearly seen once the "I am" has dissolved. That which remains is discovered to be that which
was there before the "I am" ever arose.

Despite this description, my friend insisted that the
usual notion of pure subjectivity defined it as a type of God-
consciousness that entailed a transition between ordinary
self-consciousness, and a form of divine consciousness, in
which one is aware of one's self as God. It means taking on
God's own form of Self-consciousness — supposing, of
course, that God *is* self-conscious — whereby the ordinary
self disappears when this divine Self is revealed. There is no
real identity here of subject and object because these are
transcended — left behind — and only the One remains.

Now I cannot question another man's experience; all I
can do is be honest about my own. For two people to have
different experiences that go by the same name is a common
occurrence and certainly no cause for argument. My present
concern for clarifying an understanding of pure subjectivity
is to show how it is the keystone on which self either rises or
falls. I was interested in what my friend had to say because,
with his understanding of pure subjectivity, the self surely
rises, rises to Godhood in fact; whereas in my view, the self

— be it higher or lower, divine or otherwise — falls, disintegrates, and disappears forever. These are two different views of pure subjectivity, and since I have no experience to verify the rise of the self, I must leave this to others and move on to show how, for me, at least, there was no identification of self as God.

As I see it, the subject and object of pure subjectivity are not transcended. But to understand this, it is necessary to find out what, if possible, could be an object to the eye seeing itself that is not itself already. Unlike ordinary consciousness that knows an endless array of objects, pure subjectivity has but one object — namely, the subject. Thus it makes no difference where we look or what we do, whether we are asleep or shopping, engrossed in a book or adding up the bills, the object of the eye seeing itself (which *is* itself) is the same, day and night, moment by moment. This is no transient experience or game of now-you-see-it, now-you-don't; it is a new way of knowing not comparable to the subject-object method of ordinary consciousness.

To further account for this unusual subject and object, I must once more revert to the drawing of the star. Before its outline appeared (on paper) we did not know it existed; only the drawing enables us to know its form. But once it is drawn, the three aspects of the star become known. First, there is its unmanifested aspect before the drawing which, after the drawing, may be seen as its empty center. Second, there is the aspect of drawing itself, or the movement that made its form a visible reality. Third, there is the obvious and indisputable outline itself. Thus we have: the unmanifested or unknown; the act of manifesting; and the manifested or known. Applied to pure subjectivity, we can speak of these as the knower or subject, the knowing or mediator, and the known or object — all three existing, acting, and knowing as One. These three aspects are never transcended because they constitute the very essence of the One eye seeing itself.

If I have not made it clear before, I should emphasize that empirical reality or physical form *is* the known aspect or object in pure subjectivity. But the way this object is known is not by the usual methods of knowing. To know the object inherent in pure subjectivity is also to know the subject, since there is no psychological or mental division such as usually enables us to know something "in particular" — as separate, unique, and individual. So, despite the visual discreteness of empirical objects, wherever the eye looks it sees only itself.

Before the journey, I could look out the window and see a tree as the object of my mind and perception. Today I look out the window and see, not only the visible, manifested aspect of pure subjectivity (the tree) but I also see its invisible, unmanifested aspect; and with such an emphasis on the latter, it is only with perceptual strain that I can focus on the former. In fact, I can no longer focus on visual form alone. Where once the manifested had been seen first, now it is seen second. This does not mean that the manifested is of lesser reality; it only means it is (or at least *was*, before this journey) a gateway. It is like the crust on a loaf of bread which is not separate from its more profound depths. In this way, the unmanifested is also the manifested; they are not separate realities, but only two aspects of the One truth. The seer of this reality is not myself, and what is seen is not merely a tree; rather, seer and seen are two aspects of the eye seeing itself, which I have defined as pure subjectivity.

The object or manifested aspect of reality is ever changing, and therefore we say it is perishable. But in truth, nothing is perishable, because the unmanifested aspect (of any object) does not change even though it moves — constantly moves to manifest itself.

In my first glimpse of pure subjectivity, the gesture of the smile had these three aspects of knower, knowing, and known, that told me of a way of knowning that entailed no reflexive mechanism, had no need for objectification, and took no movement of the mind. There was nothing about this seeing (or pure subjectivity) that could either be called self-conscious or God-conscious, because the eye needed nothing within or without in order to know itself. The known is not an image or reflection of the knower; it is not an idea or an appearance in the knower's mind; and certainly it is not an illusion. Rather, the known (object) is the unknown (subject) as well as the knowing (mediator) which together form the trinitarian aspects of the One eye seeing itself. The eye has no need to be aware of itself because there is nothing that is not itself; thus, it has no reflexive mechanism and cannot be said to be self-conscious. What this means — to me at least — is that pure subjectivity lies outside and beyond all consciousness.

Nevertheless, because we find the same three aspects of seer, seeing, and seen, as features of all consciousness (though in a less pure form) we can easily make the mistake of equating two entirely different ways of knowing. It is a great error, I think, to identify pure subjectivity as any form of self-consciousness; even if these two ways of knowing appear intellectually and logically analogous, the fact remains that on an experiential level, they are totally incompatible. If this were not the case — if they were compatible, then no transition would be necessary. This journey then, is not a transition between self-consciousness and God-consciousness, nor did it culminate in any knowledge equating self and God.

At the end of the first movement, however, there is a type of God-consciousness wherein we are as much aware of the still-point at the center of our being as we are aware of ourselves; thus, we know we are part and parcel of God and a run-on with the Divine, but this type of consciousness still belongs to the self; it is not pure subjectivity. Strictly speaking then, the transition of the second movement may not be a transition in consciousness at all; though an obvious change in consciousness takes place, the major transition is the discovery of a new way of knowing and seeing that goes beyond anything we call consciousness, and certainly beyond anything we could call "self."

Unless pure subjectivity is known as an immediate experience, there may be no way to understand it. Even after it is experienced, it may still not be adequately understood; and in my case, even when it had been both experienced and understood, it was still not easy to accept. The reason for this difficulty was because God-as-object died hard, so hard in fact, it was not entirely dead after both knowing and experiencing that as an object, God was no longer available.

It was the disintegration of God-as-object, not the disappearance of the self, that proved to be the most difficult and bewildering aspect of the journey. While the self had become nothing but a stillness and silence within, the automatic mental or psychological movement of my mind to focus on God as an object went right on, and toward the end of the journey became a peculiar type of problem. It seems that trying to make God an object was the last and final unconscious movement of my mind to be put to rest. As an object, God was an unquestioned certitude, an immediate knowledge like the most basic fact of life. As said before, I knew God as well as I knew myself — which doesn't say much, but at least it says something.

Prior to the journey, God had not been an object in the sense of being completely "other" to myself. I looked upon Him as part and parcel of my true self, the completion of my wholeness as an individual and the very core of my being. In this way God was an aspect of my own subjectivity, but an aspect I could still focus on, or sink to, by an interior movement of love, or whatever faculty it was that enabled me to be aware of God as the still-point within. It was as if God were half-subject half-object, and in this union I felt most secure. It was a knowledge and security born of the first movement and sustained for over twenty years, or until this journey — the second movement — began.

In the years between those two movements I sometimes had experiences in which the line of separation between self and God seemed to disappear, and though I searched myself, could not come upon any clear knowledge or certitude regarding what was His and what was mine. This was not so much the experience of loss of self as the loss of a clear-cut line of demarcation. At first these experiences were few and far between, but later they grew closer together, until it became a cause for concern when I seemed to come to a permanent and quite natural state in which a division between self and God was no longer apparent. Once the line of separation disappears there is no "other," there is no self, and though life went on as usual, I had no certitude of who was living it — God or myself. To be lost and dissolved in God was highly desirable, but to be lost and dissolved in nothing knowable — as is God-as-subject — was not, in my opinion, the way things should go.

Looking back from my present perspective, I now see what I failed to see at the time: with the loss of self there is also a loss of God-as-object. These two, self and God-as-object, are so intimately bound together we cannot possibly lose one without losing the other; yet, this never dawned on me until after both losses had become an accomplished fact.

But before this happened, I did not cling to my self in the need for individual autonomy, since I knew I was totally dependent upon God anyway. What I clung to was the line of separation, because it is only a sense of separation that makes it possible for God to be an object to the self. Since I had always taken this division for granted, I was all the more amazed and disconcerted when it (the line, so to speak) disappeared. Those who would tell us that God is all that remains when the division between God and self is no longer apparent, may be speaking prematurely, because on an experiential level, God is not what we think He is or will be. When first seen, He may not be recognized or known at all. Thus, finding out what remains in the absence of self is the pearl of great price, a long journey, a change of consciousness, and the beginning of a new life.

Even at the end of the journey, and with my first glimpses of pure subjectivity, I thought that although God-as-subject was, without a doubt, the highest truth ever encountered, its seeing and knowledge brought about less human satisfaction than knowing God-as-object. As an object, God is hard to beat. He is the object of our love, our will, and our desires; with or without an image, he is the object of our minds and feelings; he is the object we see in others and in all of nature; he is our constant companion and other half; he is the one we look for in every relationship. And having seeen this object all my life, it seemed terrible and unnecessary for God to do away with such a consoling and meaningful factor in human existence. I could never have done away with God-as-object because I could never have stopped my faculties from looking for this — their true object.

Consequently, I regarded pure subjectivity as a passing foretaste of the way God would be known after death, and tried to put it aside as not belonging to a permanent way of knowing in the here and now. But what I went on to discover was that God-as-subject could not be put aside anymore than God-as-object could be made to take its place. This then, was the peculiar dilemma I encountered at the end of the journey: the dilemma of being subtly cornered between two ways of knowing in which the choice was not mine to make.

It took many overwhelming and lasting experiences of pure subjectivity to finally realize its total relevance in the here and now. The initial experiences were a combination of possession, revelation, and seeing in which there was no one to be possessed, nothing for it to be revealed to, and the seeing was only a seeing of itself. It was like the stealthy obliteration of everything but the consciousness of Itself. In the last chapter I described such an experience and was mistaken to think it a passing infusion, because it turned out that what had initially been so awesome and unbelievable, gradually became a continuous clear reality. Somehow, it seemed necessary to see again and again how pure subjectivity was, itself, the now-moment, the continuous wakefulness, the concentrated wholeness, the intensity, and the great abiding certitude all of which adds up to an experiential understanding of how pure subjectivity works.

Then finally, after many months, the day came when that subtle movement — or whatever it was that persistently searched for God-as-object — disappeared, and God-as-subject came into its own. I might add, this was also the day I saw how Christ was all form, which somehow seemed responsible for putting a blessed, irrevocable end to the mind's automatic search for an object. Thereafter the mind never made the slightest movement to "look," and in this way, learned to live fully in the now-moment. All this took time, however, but then time seems to be of Its essence because God must have some measure for the events in a woman's life.

Realizing that this transition from God-as-object to God-as-subject will not be understood by everyone, I cannot leave this discussion without affirming my conviction that when it comes to living a good life, being a good person, or establishing a deep relationship with God, this transition is not really necessary. As a subject or as an object, God is God, and the only thing that changes in this transition is the way of knowing Him. God of the woods, the stillpoint and silence within, known or unknown, subject or object, it is all God, and life is just a movement toward a clearer vision. Naturally I do not know if everyone must eventually make this transition, but I would think it easier to make after death or without the interference of so many psychological and intellectual habits that tend to impede this journey in the here and now.

As I hope I have shown, empirical reality is not itself

an obstacle to seeing; rather, it is what we *think* about this reality that creates an obstacle to a transition that otherwise might not have been necessary in the first place. As it stands now, I still have a number of problems due to the continual need to compromise. I am surrounded by people with whom I need to relate; I live amid values, ideas, and opinions on which I must express myself; and because of this environment, I am continually impressed with the difficulty of sharing a journey with others who do not see as I now see. Yet this very inability, this abiding difficulty, only brings home to me the more how incomplete life is and ever will be until everyone can see.

Self

The usual method of studying the self is to view it in relation to the collective, the other, the unconscious, or whatever is designated as the not-self. My approach to this study, however, is by a different route. Because of this journey I was able to view the self as relative to its absence, or no-self; in other words, I learned what *was* when I learned what Is. Although every method of learning is by some relative means, the study of self relative to the not-self yields a different set of insights, experiences, and conclusions than when it is studied relative to no-self; and, naturally, it is only with these latter findings that I am presently concerned.

Owing to this particular approach, I must leave behind the usual theories, psychological speculations, and methods of studying the self, especially when these begin with the assumption that self is a permanent entity, an indelible fixture of human nature. My own point of departure was the sudden realization that this was not so. It is important, I think, to point out these differences because what I have to say may be incomprehensible and unacceptable to those who have taken the traditional route. In turn, I might add that I have never understood the analytical approach or scheme of the psyche; it somehow failed to recognize God as the true center of man's being and thus, on an experiential level, such an approach has ever remained foreign and incomprehensible to me.

I think it is safe to begin by saying that without the reflexive ability of the mind to bend back on itself, there
would be no thinker of thoughts, no doer of doing, no feeler
of feelings, and thus, there would be no such thing as a self.
In its own right, the reflexive mechanism of the mind is not
the self; rather, it is only a mechanism that makes self possible — I would even say, inevitable. But the mechanism enabling us to look inward and become self-conscious is the
same mechanism enabling us to look outward and become
object-conscious so that together, they form the two sides of
our ordinary subject-object consciousness necessary for an
empirical way of knowing.

If we were to deny we could look inward to study the
self as object, we would also have to deny we could look
outward to study empirical objects; therefore, because they
share the same type of consciousness, the self is as real and
factual as any piece of scientific information. Yet, like all
such information, it is provisional at best, subject to change,
and in the end, utterly perishable.

The experience that initiated this journey was the permanent silencing or closing down of the reflexive mechanism of the mind, with the result that it became impossible to
remember myself. I could no longer reflect backward or inward, and though I strove with all possible energy to remain
self-conscious, my mind kept falling back into the silence of
no-self-consciousness. When this occurred, I blacked out
because there was nothing there anymore — there was no
thinker of thoughts, no doer of doing. Not only as an object
had self disappeared, but as a self-conscious mechanism, self
had become an impossibility.

When fully conscious, however, I knew that some aspect of my mind had opened onto the Unknown in a contemplative gaze with which I was well acquainted, but a
gaze that had never been so continuously enforced or permanently focused; a gaze out of which the mind could not
move. (The Unknown is not, of course, the blackout, the

darkness, or the unconsciousness; rather, the self is all these things. Indeed, God is not the dark of the mind; self as subject is this darkness.) By allowing this gaze full rein I became used to not looking within, and in this way I was able to stay awake and overcome the continual inclination to fall back into the emptiness and void of self-consciousness.

Realizing the self was gone, I looked inward on one occasion to behold not one, but two voids, and at seeing this I felt as if my life's energy had suddenly been drained away. It was a sense of life I never knew I had because it was not connected with the mind or consciousness, nor with the body and its ordinary energies. This was not a passing experience; on the contrary, it was the onset of discovering a new life, a life wherein there was no feeling of self anymore — a life I had first to discover, and later, to adjust to.

Thus, in the first event or closing down of the reflexive mechanism, I could no longer *remember* myself; in the second event, or the withdrawal of the sense of personal energy, I could no longer *feel* myself. I believe this sequence of events to be important because, in retrospect, it enabled me to piece together this phenomenon called the self, a phenomenon which seems to disappear in the order of its initial appearance. And as to how the self arises, I will have something to say in a moment.

After these two events, and as I moved through the following weeks and months, I gradually discovered that the major result of these bewildering experiences was the disappearance of the entire affective system. It took a full year, however, before this dawned on me, and the circumstances under which it did so — the horrible void I saw on the beach — made it, initially, a hard pill to swallow. I saw myself as unwittingly trapped without a means of escape when I realized that once the self is gone, the resultant state is irreversible; the affective system could not be resurrected. In turn, this recognition was responsible for the unfelt, unknown terror and dread that afterwards came to mind. But

once it had been confronted openly on the hillside, this insane phenomenon never reappeared.

It was here I discovered that the stillness of no-self
would hold fast against the most terrifying and unknown
machinations of the mind. I learned that without any *feelings* to back it up, the mind is absolutely powerless to effect
a single thing. At the same time, it became obvious that the
stillness and silence of no-self was, indeed, a marvelous and
irreversible blessing.

Through these events I came to understand how the indefinable, almost unconscious, personal sense of subjective
energy and life was the nucleus, the tough core around
which the affective system was built; a system that not only
belongs to the self, but *is* the self. This feeling of personal
life is like a seed within that branches out to permeate every
aspect of our being. So to be without a self means to be
without this seed, this gut-level feeling of personal being,
along with all its branches, the entire affective system. In the
second event of the journey then, this seed and all to which
it had given rise was uprooted in one full sweep, like a tree
that had suddenly been felled. Life goes on, but it is a new
life, one that is neither personal nor impersonal — it is simply
a life without a self.

So this was what I discovered: that self is the entire affective emotional network of feelings, from the most subtle
unconscious stirrings of energy, to the obvious extremes of
passionate outbursts. Though separate from the cognitive
system, the affective life so infiltrates the mind and all its
processes that we can never separate our energies from the
cognitive faculties as long as the reflexive mechanism remains intact.

Ordinarily we do not realize the extent of this infiltra-
tion because we like to believe we can be purely objective at
times, when in fact we cannot. Subjectivity and objectivity
are two sides of the same coin — the same type of consciousness — and though the cognitive structure remains in-

tact when the affective system disappears, it then functions in a different way, a way I have tried to describe in the last chapter.

To account for the rise of the affective system, we need only remember that the child *feels* long before he *thinks*. It is only gradually, with the development of the brain, that he discovers a separation exists between the seer and the seen, and with this discovery he becomes self-conscious. And once this takes place, his feelings become inseparably fused with his knowing. Thereafter both the knowledge and the feeling of self are all but indistinguishable. When the self disappears, this *knowledge* and *feeling* of a self disappear together like twin systems of a single circuit.

Because feeling precedes self-consciousness, it should be noted that the mere acknowledgment of self as an object of consciousness is insufficient to account for the self's existence. Without a sense of personal energy or feeling to back it up, such knowledge is so lifeless and meaningless, it is no more than a mental construct as easily dispelled as a child's belief in Santa Claus. The self is more than a knowledge of its own existence, and what this more is, is a gut-level feeling of energy, drive, power, and of a will that, when linked with the cognitive faculties, becomes the subjective certitude "this is me." This energy permeates our thoughts, words, and deeds to such an extent that we have come to believe these feelings are part and parcel of what it means to be human — a belief I now see is a great mistake.

Although the feeling of personal energy — which, in the early years, is indistinguishable from the sensation of simple *physical* energy — precedes the conscious knowledge "this is me," I think it is obvious that the self only becomes a force when self-consciousness — which *is* the reflexive mechanism — develops to the point of claiming this physical energy for its own. Thus, no matter how much physical energy a man has, without this self-conscious mechanism there could be no feeling of *personal* energy. Without a sense of possession, physical energy has no more meaning, no more feeling behind it, than the noticeable effects of air and water to which no one can make a personal claim.

When the reflexive mechanism closes down, however, the feeling of physical energy again becomes separated from self-consciousness, and though this energy remains, it cannot be experienced in the same possessive way as it was before. Cut off from self-consciousness, the knowledge and feeling of getting around under our own steam is gone. At first this gives way to something akin to a sense of weightlessness, an unusual type of knowledge (not really a physical sensation) that will remain with us as long as any relative difference between the old way of *feeling* life and the new way of *knowing* life can be noticed or recalled. As we acclimate to this new life, the old ways of feeling energy are quickly forgotten, or so I learned from experience.

In the history of the self then, physical energy comes first. Self-consciousness comes next, and develops to the point of becoming aware of physical energy within the body, which it then claims as its own. In this way, the reflexive mechanism of the mind, which is not the self, nevertheless gives rise to the self or makes it possible. But with this recognition of personal energy, a division is created between what was initially physical energy, and what we will now call "self-energy," will, or mental, psychic energy, which some people believe is beyond the physical realm — and in some ways it is. Where at first there was only energy of the body, now there is energy of the mind, which resulted when the sense of personal energy infiltrated the cognitive system seemingly to energize its thoughts and acts. It goes without saying that, of itself, thought has no power or meaning unless there is some force or drive to back it up. Rid thought of this power, and thinking appears to be no more than a neurological mechanism of the brain. Ultimately then, self is not the thinker of thoughts; rather, at its most subtle, rock-bottom level, self is nothing more, yet nothing less, than the *consciousness of "personal" energy.*

Given this history, it should be obvious that if someone wanted to go beyond the self, it would be useless to try
to alter either the cognitive or affective systems. As long as
the brain persists with its automatic reflexive mechanism, it
would only bring about another self no matter how we try
to suppress or tamper with these systems. So whatever the
reflexive mechanism is, it is strategic both to a life with a self
and a life without a self. This is why I have said that only an
outside agent can bring about the demise of the self; an
agent, however, that has a physiological counterpart. I am
convinced that we may some day discover the secret of this
reflexive mechanism and in doing so, we will have discovered
the difference between man and beast. A premature cut-off of
this mechanism could prove more damaging to human life
than anything man has yet devised for its destruction.

Nevertheless, when the time is ripe — a time no man
knows of — this mechanism gives out, gives way to a life
that is beyond any need of a self. This does not mean we fall
back into an infantile or bestial form of life. Though we
continue to share in every strata of existence, the disintegration of the self is a forward, not a backward, movement.
Once the mind has been appropriately conditioned to its
human potential, it does not forfeit this in order to see "that"
which lies beyond it.

The impermanence of the self is comparable, perhaps,
to the pineal body or organ in the center of the brain, which
is said to be functional in the developmental years but later
ceases to function. In similar fashion, the self, which was
necessary for a specific way of knowing in the first part of
life, ceases to function when it has outgrown its usefulness.
Thus, the intervention of an outside agent has something to
do with man's reaching an unknown level of psychological
development, integration, or evolution, before this agent
can act, or before man can dare to live without a self. Indeed, the very need for integration is to come to a point of

graceful disintegration; the need for personal wholeness is to pass into a greater wholeness; and the purpose of having a self is to eventually go beyond it.

The knowledge of individual wholeness and unity realized before the journey began, is akin, though not identical to, the wholeness that remains when the journey is over, or when there is no self. Once we pass over the line, it becomes possible to realize a greater wholeness than that of individual being, which is the wholeness of all that Is. The unity of the self has disappeared, disintegrated, and given way to a wholeness that has no parts and therefore cannot be said to be integrated. Nevertheless, it was the initial integration that constituted the necessary preparation for the journey, and without it, I do not see how the passage could be made. To have no-self, there must first *be* a self — a whole self.

In recent years we have begun to explore the process of integration, but it will undoubtedly be a long time before we get around to investigating the process of disintegration; and for now, at least, I know of no one who even admits to such a possibility. Perhaps this study will come about through the efforts to extend our knowledge of the aging process. But as it stands now, it seems the self is regarded as an eternally divine necessity from birth to death — and into the beyond. It is this refusal to look beyond that makes the usual study of self such a closed system of investigation; and this refusal, like every unquestioned assumption, turns out to limit, confine, and eventually entrap us, when it leaves no door open to change, or to that which lies beyond the system itself.

O

Now that we have seen that the core of self is a sense of personal energy, we must go on to say something of the branches to which this seed gives rise: the entire affective system, which includes not only the emotions, but feelings we do not ordinarily associate with the system at all. What follows then, is what I know of this system, based not only upon what I discovered during the journey, but upon much that I learned before it began.

Since the affective system is on a single relative continuum, I look upon it as a seesaw, where the ends of the board (or continuum) represent the extremes of attraction and repulsion, and the area closest to the near immovable center represent its more subtle, often unconscious, movements.

Supposing that the fulcrum on which this continuum rests is the cognitive system, we can see that the process of integration is a balancing act wherein the ultimate goal is maintaining an equilibrium against all forces to the contrary. The greatest force acting against this balance comes from the extremities of the continuum; the most subtle forces closest to the center, are responsible for our first spontaneous movements in either direction.

Obviously, optimum stability is achieved at the center of the two systems, a center wherein the contemplative eventually discovers maximum access to the still-point — which is a point not *of* the system but discoverable through it. In fact, the contemplative's sole reason for desiring this stability or unity between systems is because the silent, quiet, near immovable center of the continuum (self or affective system) is the gateway to the true center of his being — the still-point. Thus, where the equilibrium sought by the non-contemplative is only between the two systems themselves, the contemplative seeks an alignment between these systems and the still-point — once again, not to be confused with the near immovable center of the affective system.

I cannot say for certain if the center of the affective system is actually immovable; all I know is that this center is where the contemplative makes contact with God. It goes without saying, of course, that God is not immovable, much less a still-point; these terms are simply the language of experience and do not attempt to define God. Therefore, the still-point refers to that experiential unlocalized "spot" in ourselves where man runs into God. For man's part, this spot seems to be at the center of the affective continuum which, I might add, does not appear to be dependent upon the fulcrum below.

The contemplative is continually scanning this continuum looking for its stillest point, but often cannot find it; therefore, the still-point, when it can be seen, acts like a beacon on which the contemplative focuses his gaze and, in doing so, is pulled like a magnet toward this center wherein the affective system comes to a standstill. In this way, the still-point acts as the greatest inhibitor of the affective continuum that we know of; it gradually immobilizes all movements along the continuum by bringing them to rest in an undisturbable sense of peace, silence, and stillness. Above all, it rests in the certitude of Its presence.

As an inexperienced contemplative, I noticed how I often ruined this sense of presence by becoming so emotional about it that God was overshadowed and effaced by the extremes of my reactions. I knew I had to be still, but by my own efforts could not do this. When I tried to ignore this presence, to let it be, to make nothing out of it, this worked better; but unfortunately it doesn't work the other way around. We can ignore God, but he can no more ignore us than he can cease to exist, and because he exists he touches us, and for this reason I made little progress in my efforts to maintain the necessary interior stillness.

It was only after the dark night of the soul, wherein a shift occurred between God as a sensible, *felt* presence, to God as a *knowable*, seeable (but veiled) presence, that I was able to make continuous contact with the still-point without an affective overflow. At the same time I discovered — to my relief — that I could no longer experience the extremes of the continuum, because after this night nothing was able to alter the deep sense of peace, stillness, and strength at the center of myself. But if the board no longer dipped to extremes, it continued to go up and down. For years, this inner core of "all is well" was tested by a great variety of exterior (not interior) forces that tried to move the imperturbable center. At times I wondered what kept me from sliding off the deep end, but at the last minute the still-point would open up, expand, and draw everything into its silence.

After many years and long practice on this beam, I knew I had gradually edged my way to the center, or close enough so that none of my responses to life's events went beyond spontaneous first movements; movements, however, that could as well be in one direction as another. Because they were so automatic and spontaneous, these movements seemed not to be under my control, and about this, I was highly skeptical. I never cared for instinctual living, and ever chose my head over my emotions. Then too, I had little trust in any aspect of the affective system since it never taught me the truth about anything. I knew better than to base any faith, hope, or charity on how I felt that day. For these reasons I looked upon such spontaneous movements as a peculiar impasse to absolute stillness. Though harmless in themselves, I found these movements more mystifying than anything encountered before, because I was not sure if they were of myself, of God, or of some unknown instinctual force. Finally I decided they represented a gap between myself and God, a mysterious dividing line, an impasse I could not see my way around. But by adopting a wait-and-see attitude I was able to come to the point of watching these movements without acting on them. It was while watching that I made a curious discovery.

The gap between the near immovable center of the continuum and the still-point turned out to be a battleground for two opposing forces, forces that were not between the affective extremes or between the two systems themselves, but two mysterious forces that, strangely, seemed to have nothing to do with me whatsoever.

On one occasion, I had the unique experience of quietly

observing this battle rage within myself without being touched in any way. Here, for the first time I asked myself: who is watching this? who is this outside observer? Naturally, I had no answer. When the battle dissolved, I took for granted some issue had been settled, but having no idea what this was, I put the incident aside as yet another mystery of the contemplative life.

Shortly after, I understood this battle and realized that what we usually think of as good and evil are actually the forces of self-preservation and self-extinction. The line between them is like a gate that the preserving forces would close to anyone going beyond, while the forces for extinction are the power that keeps the gate open. It was after this battle that I realized the impasse had been removed. The instinctive, spontaneous first-movements on the continuum were gone, and I came upon the clear possibility of making a more complete alignment with the still-point. What happened when the alignment was made is the story of this journey, a journey that not only went beyond all affective movements, but beyond the continuum itself.

In this way, the still-point gradually drew this system into its silence, and once the stillness was complete, the continuum was no more, the self was no more, and being relative to these, the still-point was no more. Union with God then, is not complete until there is nothing left to be united. Between the self (the still center on the affective continuum) and God (the still-point) there is no gap remaining. What is left is what Is, all that Is, and Its identity is unmistakable.

A friend recently told me that the falling away of the affective system was invariably a psychotic symptom. While I had never heard this before and have no idea if it's true, my present perspective is quite the opposite. As I see it, the affective system is not only the cause of every psychological illness, it is the cause of *all* man's suffering. An organic problem, without this system, could not give way to psychological or mental suffering, because there would be no fears, anxieties, or all the rest that so easily erupt into emotional disturbances.

In keeping with this is the admission of a gentleman who said he was terrified at the thought of losing his self. What he had obviously failed to realize was that the terror and dread he felt *is* the self, and that without a self there can be no such feelings. In fact, a sure sign the self is gone is the absence of these affective symptoms. So as long as there is any fear of losing the self, the self remains — in which case there is nothing to worry about one way or the other. But this is why the histories of those who have truly gone beyond the self will never be found in psychiatric literature. With no problems in the affective domain, few people would be in need of a psychiatrist or analyst; indeed, without an affective system, or without a self, this whole school of thought would be out of business.

Yet we cling to the affective system out of fear of what life would be like without it. We're afraid that without feelings we will be inhuman, cold, insensitive, robot-like creatures, so detached from this world that we might as well be dead. Needless to say, there is no truth in this view at all; it is just another myth created out of fear of the unknown — where all myths come from. Nevertheless, to explain what life is like without this system is not easy because it must be lived to be understood, and any description of it only gives rise to an unending chain of philosophical arguments. All that need be said here is that it is a dynamic, intense state of caring; caring for whatever arises in the now-moment. It is a continuous waking state in which the physical organism remains sensitive, responsive, and totally unimpaired. When the journey is over, nothing is found to be missing or wanting. It is only in the encounter with other selves that a self — or affective system — is seen as a continuous reminder of what *was*.

One of the reasons such a state is difficult to understand is that few people realize, within themselves, the full extent of what the affective system really is. Some people think of it as the loving heart in man when, actually, this is but a fraction of its reality. A far larger part consists of the only true diabolical force in existence and, unfortunately, these affective extremes are not far apart — they're only relative one to the other. A way out of this dilemma of relativity would be to live on only half the beam — the good half, that is — but it doesn't work this way; either we are potentially subject to all these movements or we are subject to none of them. Some movements, however, are so subtle, we think of them — mistakenly — as primarily cognitive, or sometimes as merely physical, and since filtering out this system from the rest of our being is so impossible, we seek integration as a way of at least keeping it in line.

It is imperative to examine closely and realize that the root of the affective system is a sense of selfhood; a feeling of personal being which is identical to its will, its drives, motivations, values, and goals. This branches out to give rise to memories, desires, expectations. This fans out still further to color every perception and thought, until it reaches into every experience including the aesthetic sense of beauty, a sense of natural order, a sense of contentment, peace, boredom, tiredness, loneliness, *ad infinitum*. In a word, this system includes every sense of psychological interiority, and feeling of contemplative spirituality, that we know of.

Because the self is all this and so much more, any description of what remains when it falls away is bound to raise questions of a moral, behavioral, relational, and even of a metaphysical nature. Without a self there arises the question: what becomes the standard of measurement for the good life, right action, decisions, values and so on? To say there is no standard is to say the incomprehensible, but also to say the truth; a truth, however, that is only relative to having no self. Before coming to this state, standards must exist because it is the nature of the self to create them, and then to live by them.

It is difficult to understand an effortless, choiceless state that needs no standard to survive. The mind cannot grasp this realm of the non-relative, a realm that has nothing to do with the fusion of opposites or the maintenance of a balance between the poles of differences and variations. This state is nothing more than a simple straightforward look at what Is, a look that can no longer scan a continuum that doesn't exist, for options that do not exist. Nor does it look backward or forward because in the now-moment each moment is sufficient unto itself. It is impossible to step outside this moment wherein there is no choice and no standard.

It was this non-relative dimension I found missing when searching through the contemplative literature for insight into this particular state. Since self is a sense of interiority, the criteria of my search for this second contemplative movement was the absence of an interior life — which, of course, I did not find. Instead, I encountered the usual descriptions of love and bliss, lights and energies, God within and the true self, all of them descriptive of the first movement, and all of them belonging to the purely relative affective system.

I understood some of these experiences, but had to discount them as belonging to the present movement. I found no one who admitted or even suggested the complete falling away of the affective life. At most it seems that only its negative aspects are said to disappear, and it was this fact I found most questionable. If we are to live permanently at the positive affective pole, I do not see the possibility of a balanced life, nor do I see the impossibility of sooner or later experiencing a dip in the opposite direction. With the exception of the near immovable center, every point or movement on the continuum is relative to some other movement; thus, as long as the system exists we can never get beyond the relativity of our experiences. Feelings of love, bliss, joy, and all things ineffable are merely relative to their opposite, their absence, or some other point along the continuum; so when I encountered these descriptions I knew they were not what I was looking for. They were not indicative of the second movement beyond the self.

It occurred to me that the falling away of the affective life might be a piece of esoteric knowledge not given to the outsider, or even to the proficient, because he would not understand it ahead of time, and as a future prospect, it could prove frightening. So as it stands now, the high contemplative goal is generally regarded as a state of uninterrupted bliss or ecstatic union, which has become the incentive and the expectation.

With regard to both movements this is nonsense, of course, but more especially when it is applied to the second non-relative movement that knows no such descriptions of interiority. More to the point in accounting for this non-relative state would be a description of the new life: "what is," and how it works. I would even characterize it as a tough and restrictive condition because it is centered in a stillness out of which it cannot move. At the same time, this state is fluid because it knows no rules and laws of order; it has no standards. Outside this state, however, lies the plane of relativity, synonomous with subjectivity, obstruction, indefiniteness and vagueness, for which reason it strives mightily to find laws and principles to govern what is. Obviously the affective life fills this prescription.

For all this it could be said, nevertheless, that the affective system is a fairly sturdy tree of personal life in which every mature adult eventually feels at home. If there is any problem with this tree it is that some of its fruit is good and some of it is not so good, and as long as the tree remains productive, there is the potential for yielding either kind. This is the risk involved, the price to be paid for the knowledge that makes scientific and cultural achievements possible; but however much we are indebted to the good fruit, there is nothing eternal about this tree. At best, it is a temporary mechanism for developing a certain type of intelligence, an intelligence we must eventually learn to live without; if not now, then later.

Perhaps the most relevant questions to be asked regarding the falling away of the affective system would be these. What takes the place of its better aspects, or how are we to account for charity, sympathy, compassion, and love? And, how would it be possible to look upon the non-relative as a "better" state if it is lacking in such virtues?

For someone who has made the passage, these questions do not arise because such a person is not aware of the absence of virtue. What is absent, however, is the need to *practice* virtue. What remains after the passage is not unkind, un-understanding, condemning, or any of the rest; so the need to practice virtue does not arise. What before we had to strive for, or put there, is now "there" of its own accord as if it were the most natural thing in the world.

But if these questions are not relevant to the state itself, they will invariably arise in its description, and at one point these questions were put to me in a manner I did not, at first, understand.

When handing back my account, a religious friend said to me, "What I want to know is how you think this journey changed you? What were its effects? In what way are you different now?" His questions took me by surprise because to tell the truth, I thought I'd said it all. I thought the changes that took place were so obvious that despite my lack of talent, the events alone had somehow told the story. With his queries, however, I saw my mistake and realized that though I should write forever, I could never make clear to others the changes that were so obvious to me. Recently someone passed on to me a Hindu saying to the effect: those who say they see, do not see, because those who see, say nothing. I can now add to this: even those who say they see, say nothing. Thus, whether we speak up or say nothing, it makes no difference.

My friend's questions, however, stuck in my mind. I was continually thinking of all the things I hadn't said — and there's quite a lot of that — but none of it, I thought, *apropos* to his questions. Finally I decided that since he was a religious individual, he must have been referring to the usual standard of Christian measurement: by their fruits you shall know them. So the questions become: am I a better person — a better Christian? am I more charitable? do I love God more? am I more virtuous? and so on. Although the idea of answering "no" to all this strikes me as particularly wicked, this must nevertheless be my answer, because in more ways than these even, there is nothing to show for having taken this journey. In fact there is less to see now than before, because the very occasions that once arose for the practice of virtue no longer arise. This does not imply the absence of good; it only means that as a practice, virtue is absent. The key to understanding this lies, I believe, in the fact that the will, which provides the power and drive to put virtue and vice into motion, has disappeared.

If it has not been underscored before, it must be emphasized here, that the faculty of the will is itself, the core of the affective system, the seed of the self, and the feeling of personal energy that gives rise to the system in the first place. Thought alone is powerless to act because it must be moved by this feeling if it is to have any part in our behaviors. This then, was the major discovery regarding the self: that its very nucleus *is* the will or volitional faculty.

Though I had been taught that the will was a cognitive and not an affective faculty, I was never able to place it in either category — at least experientially — since it was somehow superior and more mysterious than either of these faculties. What I see now, however, is that the will is not truly associated with the cognitive, for the ordinary faculties of the mind continue undisturbed in its absence. I also see how the will is difficult to pinpoint if it is the instigator and controller of the affective system, as well as the mysterious medium between mind and feelings. When the affective system first disappears, it is not the emotions that abruptly fall away; rather, it is the very source of their power that is made immovable. As a result, the affective branches slowly fade and disappear before we even know they are gone.

It is said that union with God is a union of the will, and since the will *is* the self, we can see that when it permanently disappears into the still-point, the entire affective system is uprooted, cut off, and forever silenced. To some extent the whole drama of the journey centers on the immobility of the will or source of personal energy. Thus, from one perspective at least, all this passage really is, is the process of acclimating to a life without this faculty. Though it does no harm to retain the notion that the will is a cognitive faculty, I think those who aspire to complete their union with God had best be prepared — in the long run — to learn otherwise. In any event, this may explain why, beyond the personal tree of life, there are no fruits: no virtue and no vice.

Living in the now-moment there is no question of how we feel or should feel; there is no conflict, struggle, or practice of anything because this moment allows for no movements backward or forward, either in time or along the continuum. Somehow each moment contains within itself the appropriate action for each tiny event in life without the need for thought or feeling. This is why, perhaps, a non-relative state raises so many philosophical and theological questions. It is not understandable on an intellectual basis; it is beyond the logic, the theory and the practices that we once took for granted would last forever. Apart from the immediate experience — if it can be called that — there is nothing that can be known or observed of this state; it cannot be seen for the looking — there is nothing to see.

I must say I have always found the Christian standard of measurement somewhat questionable when it relies on the subjective judgment and opinions of others, which are often more questionable in themselves than what is observed. Of those who witnessed the good works of Christ, for example, some thought he performed these works through the power of the devil, and others thought his behavior insane. There was no consensus about this man; by his fruits alone, he was *not* known. There is a different way of knowing him, however; a hidden, personal way of understanding his identity through our own identity with God. And without this, it would be impossible to know him.

I would even go so far as to say that when it comes to knowing others, I would not greatly trust what a person had to say about himself because words are as limited to the speaker as they are to the interpreter. This may sound skeptical, but I am convinced there is yet another way, a better way of knowing others, a way that in some respects, doesn't entail knowing them at all.

To understand how this works, it may be necessary to move beyond our usual way of knowing, move to a non-relative plane where it seems, at first, a contradiction exists. Without a self, there is also no other, and therefore no relationship. How then is it possible to know others at all? To ask it another way: how can we love our neighbor as ourself when there is no self, no other, and no affective love? Before answering this I would like to explain why — for me at least — there were no changes in relationships either during or after the journey; why this was one aspect of life that remained unaffected by stepping over the line into a new way of knowing. To do this I must first say how others were known prior to the passage, since this is all that is really needed for an explanation.

My first intimations of a way of knowing others — apart from mere empirical appearances — occurred early in life when listening to a discussion at the dinner table one evening. My father had begun by quoting what a Jesuit had to say on child-rearing practices, in which he compared the infant to the vegetative stage of life. He didn't get very far, however, before Mother interrupted. "Don't quote him to me," she said. "He didn't have any!" With that, the discussion was closed. But the conversation that followed was more interesting.

It seems that mother never mistook her babes for peas

and carrots. On the contrary, she claimed she could see the Divine shining through the innocent eyes of the infant, a vision, she said, that never left once it had been seen. Now I understood this as a miraculous feat that Mother could see in me what I could not see in myself, and took for granted that one had first to be a mother before one could see this phenomenon, this vision of God in others. Later on, of course, I realized that one can only see in others what one has first seen in herself.

Mother's philosophy of life was based on seeing into the inner self. If I went to her complaining I was bored, had no one to play with, or whatever the childhood grievance, she would remind me never to be dependent upon anything outside myself for my happiness. Joy and contentment, she would say, are only found within and it is there we must look for it — find it. Looking outside ourselves we might think for a while we have found it, but it won't last. For our happiness therefore, we were not to depend upon other people, material possessions, or ever setting our heart on anything to the extent we would be heartbroken if our expectations were not fulfilled. She also stressed that we must learn how to enjoy being alone and spending time by ourselves. To live this way, she added, we must first develop our inner resources so that no matter what happened in life, we could go right on as if nothing had happened. This then, was Mother's philosophy of life, suitable to every circumstance and propounded to us with numerous variations.

On a conscious level, I never took on this way of thinking. To some extent I didn't have to because much of what she said was part of growing up. No one had to tell me I was independent or that I had to make my way in life or find my own happiness. Yet, as I grew older, I realized what a gold mine Mother had tapped within herself, and that the real challenge of being independent was just this: tapping the inner resources. But it was due to this early perspective that I somehow — albeit unconsciously — managed to skip over the problem of relationships, because to be dependent upon others was, quite simply, beyond my expectations. Furthermore, what I learned to value in others *was* their independence, since it was the first thing I valued in myself.

For some individuals, however, it seems that the overriding concern or philosophy of life is that it consists of relationships, a perspective in which everything is seen as relational, interdependent, and necessary for personal survival. This view places great emphasis on the I and the not-I as being necessary for human fulfillment. Naturally, relationships will be the major concern — and the major problem as well. Since this view is so foreign to me I can say little about it, but it seems obvious that if we try to complete ourselves by going out to the other (the not-I) before turning inward to the true "Other," we are making a wrong turn — a tragic mistake.

It is only when we realize our oneness with the true Other that we come upon a unity and wholeness that can withstand the test of all encounters with other selves. In this way, no matter what happens in our relations with the outside world, we are not fragmented, we do not fall apart, become lost, dependent, or see problems where there are none. It is only after we come upon the Other — the stillpoint at the center of our being — that we find the key to a powerful sense of security and independence that *then* allows us to go out to others, to be generous, to give them their freedom, to be open-minded and understanding. If for some reason we do not find this inner resource, we have no choice but to grasp at what is without, and it is this premature movement outward instead of inward that gives rise to all problems in relationships. The real problem in life is not between people, but between the individual and his true Other.

But let us say we have found our wholeness in God, what then is our relationship with others? Since what we see and love in others is only what we see and love in ourselves, it follows that having found God within, we can now love others as we love ourselves — love in them the same Other we have found in ourselves. And since love of God is beyond the affective system (or so I thought before this journey) so too is our love for others.

As a child, I once asked my father how it was that I felt more love for my dog than I did for God? He laughed and replied, "What you feel is called 'puppy love,' but love for God is a strong will not to offend him." Later, in discussing this emotional love versus love for God, I came to the conclusion that although the emotions may be the effect of love, they are not love *per se*. Basically then, love for others is a strong will not to hurt them, as well as desiring for them the same good we desire for ourselves. Thus, I was convinced at an early age that love was not an emotion, and as I moved through a lifetime of experiences, I never learned anything to the contrary.

Such a non-emotional basis of love will not be understood by everyone, yet it is easy to see how problems arise in relationships when love is based on our emotions. I have met individuals who cannot form a lasting friendship apart from emotional involvement and attachment, where the other is expected to reflect like a mirror their moods, humors, ideas, and schemes, and if the other does not respond in like manner, they go elsewhere, find someone else. Nevertheless, seeing God in others is not the same as seeing him in ourselves because, where our seeing is an immediate subjective movement inward, to see him in others we move outward to see the individual first and God second. But once seen, God is that quality in another that forever remains indefinable, untouchable, can never be possessed, or even adequately communicated.

This then was my outlook on the "other" and relationships before the journey began, and why, with the falling away of the affective system, there were no changes in personal relationships; although there was, in fact, a change in the way of knowing others. Where before, I had seen the individual first, and his true Other second, now the Other is seen first. And the individual? Well, I do not see him at all — not at least as before. Instead of a self I see ideas, behaviors, decisions, struggles, and much more, but I do not see a self because it has paled, effaced by what is really there.

Once again, we can only see in others what we see in ourselves; so when there is no self within, there is no self without — which is why there are no others and no relationships on a non-relative plane. Empirically it may be true that no man is an island, but beyond this level, multiplicity fades away leaving only the One. On the empirical level of differences, relations continue to exist, but exist without problems because even here, we are aware of an intrinsic bond between all that exists; so, although it is veiled, the non-relative Oneness exists on every level we know of.

My eldest son objects to the notion that beneath the façade of individual differences we are all the same. His idea is that each individual is eternally unique despite his oneness with God. I can understand this repugnance to the notion of sameness; it somehow gives the idea that God is boring, static, without variety, and that our individual differences don't count for a thing. But when saying that beyond the limitations of empirical form all things are essentially the same, I refer only to the fact that God is all that exists; I do not refer to *what* God is, what he does, or how he works. To realize that all form is made of the same clay does not subtract from the variety of form or its individual nature and behavior; on the contrary, the sameness and difference, the one and the many is, itself, the uniqueness and very essence of God and all that exists.

This alone tells us that the self cannot possibly account for our individuality. We have only to look at nature to see that the trees, the clouds, and animals do not have a self and yet are the very essence of variety and differentiation. Self does not constitute true individuality because this essential uniqueness remains when the self is gone.

It is the affective system that gives rise to the feelings, "this is my being, my life, my individuality" and on and on; but without a self there are no such feelings of possession or mistaken identity, Once we see what Is we realize: that which is different is also that which is the same. And as for the fear of losing the distinctiveness of empirical form, it takes but a single glimpse of what lies beyond this form to see that an even more unique, moving, dynamic life is but a step away. One glimpse of this new life and our present existence becomes boring, static, and insufficiently diversified by comparison. But once we see this, we are ready to move on.

Altogether then, this is what I learned about the self. To be human, man must have a self because it is part of the subject-object type of consciousness necessary for survival. It is a protective mechanism against physical death and a state of unknowing. And for a time, at least, this is the way it was meant to be. We did not fashion our own humanity any more than we fashioned air and water. We are not of our own doing. We did not give ourselves this consciousness nor fashion for ourselves an affective system or a self. All considered, human responsibility for what we *really* are, is so small and the choices so limited, it amounts to little more than the effort to avoid colliding with other objects.

I never chose my experiences as a child, never chose to go through either of the movements that have been discussed, and I know that no matter what the circumstances of life, this movement would have gone its own way. Outside our choosing and doing them, all is being moved by an unknowable intelligence, moved in one sure direction, and changing as it goes, wherein the goal is nothing more than the movement itself. Thus, we move in and out of a variety of existences, different ways of knowing and being, always changing, always moving, and this movement is our delight, our revelation, and our very life.

In this passage we encounter much that is beautiful and awesome, but as each step unfolds, we let go of the present and move into the new without clinging to what is passing. In the effort to go against the flow, we hold onto our insights, ideas, and experiences, thinking each one is the last, only to discover we must move on, taking nothing with us because what is essential at one time is accidental at another, and it is change that is life's movement.

At one point in this journey, self comes forth, contributes what it can give, then fades forever beyond reach. Self then, is part of this movement, a part through which all men must pass, and the only aspect of the movement for which man alone is responsible. But just as everything must change, the self too eventually disintegrates and dissolves into nothingness. The only thing we know that never changes or passes away is the movement Itself.

As I see it, a contemplative is one who is aware of this movement, striving at first to go with it, but later, discovering he is being moved without effort. He abandons himself to become part of it — one with it — until finally, he realizes he has never been anything other than this movement Itself.

Conclusion

Although the library, bookstores, and other sources of inquiry yielded no enlightenment, I was not destined to make this journey alone. As it happened, after searching far and wide, I returned home to find help in my own backyard when I discovered that Lucille, my friend and neighbor, was also making this passage. Initially I had been attracted to Lucille because I regarded her as a woman of extraordinary intelligence whose dignity, strength of character, and thoughtfulness of others, spoke to me of the completed individual. Yet it wasn't until this journey that we truly found one another and, like two wanderers in the unknown, the encounter was a mutual surprise, an unexpected bonus which we interpreted as no mere coincidence.

On my way to the library one afternoon, I stopped by Lucille's house to see if she might be taking her daily walk in my direction. While getting her things together she casually asked me, "So what's new?" I replied, "I don't have a self anymore." She turned to me with a bemused smile, "You, of all people! No self?" and broke into such a hearty laughter that I had to steady her on her feet. When she stopped laughing she asked, "Now tell me, seriously, what does this mean — you have no self?" I told her I didn't know, which was why I was on my way to the library, to find out. Then she began laughing all over again, and her laughter was infectious; after all, what could be more absurd than losing your self?

As we walked along I told her about this unusual state and described some of its effects. At one point she stopped walking and turned to me, "You know," she said, "I recognize what you are describing, but I'm wondering how you know all this, because you are too young. What you are talking about is the aging process. It is a change of consciousness that is reserved for the final years. It is the last stage in life, a getting ready for a new existence — and you're too young!"

Since Lucille was eighty-five at the time, she was bewildered and a bit skeptical to find her experiences mirrored in a woman almost forty years younger. She couldn't understand how this could be and, naturally, I didn't understand it myself. Nevertheless I suggested that since no one knew the time or hour of death, I might pass away before she did; in which case, I had better be as equally prepared. "Anything is possible, but it's not usual," she replied; then added with motherly concern, "anyway, you're not going to die!" With that, we linked arms tightly and went on our way.

In the next two years of sharing this journey, we were repeatedly struck by the similarity of our experiences, by our individual but similar descriptions, and even by the similarity of the coping mechanisms we had devised in the process — she was continually giving me lessons on how to remember I was forgetful. She told me of her "compensations" — as she called the seeing of "It" which I called Oneness — and of the times she too, had "turned away" because of its overwhelming intensity. In the Passageway, where I felt myself to be walking on the brink of insanity, she thought of herself as walking on the "verge of senility." And where I felt my mind to be in a vise, she described it as a caul. Since it would be impossible to recount all of her experiences, let it suffice to say that almost step by step, what I have described of this journey belongs equally to Lucille.

If there was any noticeable difference, it was that her "self," as she told me, had gradually fallen away over a period of six years or more; it had not fallen away abruptly, as in my case. Also, our major concern or emphasis was different. From beginning to end, my concern was the mystery of what remained in the absence of self; whereas for Lucille, the mystery lay in just how much of her self she could live without. She never doubted for a moment, however, that when everything was gone, when everything had been "shed," God would be all that remained — but then, according to her, life would be over. Although my view was not quite the same, the truth is, neither of us had any answers; yet we shared our unknowing, and this sharing was exciting and, at times, indescribably beautiful for we were convinced we were sharing the greatest, most important event of the human experience. Neither birth nor any experience up to this time could hold a candle to the utter reality and awesomeness of this final journey. In truth, this is where life begins!

Three years from the commencement of this journey and at this writing, Lucille, with her faculties and sense of humor intact, entered into the fullness of the new life she had discovered in this transition. Meeting her as I did at this point in my life was tremendously important because, apart from the joy of her companionship, this meeting forever dispelled any notion I may have had about this being a rare, extraordinary, mystical, or even private experience. Lucille was totally convinced this experience reflected a transition that the elderly of every generation had gone through and were going through the world over; thus it was all in the natural course of things. That I came upon this journey at an earlier age merely attests to the nature of the contemplative life, which is ever a step ahead of our ordinary, natural expectations. In fact, it is this continual running ahead that gives the contemplative life its supernatural flavor, because grace, preceding nature, is a speeding up of the natural processes; it is an advancement, like a rush on time.

This explains why the contemplative does not have to wait until middle age — as Jung would have it — before he finds his true self. This discovery is a by-product of his union with God, which can be reached at any age — even a very young age — wherein the self is completely integrated when it becomes wholly centered in God. So too, this journey beyond self does not have to wait for an advanced age; indeed, arriving at this point in mid-life illustrates, if nothing else, that man does not need a self to live by, not at this stage at least, and not forever. In this way, the supernatural exists to work in a short time what nature, so often waylaid and bogged down by irrelevancies, accomplishes over a longer period of time — and in some cases, never accomplishes at all.

Time then, is a way of accounting for the supernatural without placing it outside natural events or without the need to interpret it as something unnatural or out of the ordinary. At the same time, it is well to remember that because the natural and supernatural are equally of God's own time and making, they are on the same continuum so that, ultimately, no true separation is possible. One way or the other, God is the only one working in us for our advancement as human beings and as creatures of his own doing. Thus, whether we arrive at our final destination early or late is not, in the long run, all that relevant. Nevertheless, most of us would agree: life gets better, the sooner we get it together.

Because of my meeting with Lucille, two views of this journey became possible. One is, that the complete loss of self and the realization of what remains is a supernatural event that constitutes, for the contemplative, the second major movement of his relentless journey into God. The other view is, that this journey is the final process of our natural lifespan, wherein self-consciousness is gradually relinquished as we come upon "that" which lies beyond the self. But either way, it is a preparation for a new existence, an entry into a new way of knowing and seeing that is truly the greatest of all man's beginnings, and in no way an ending.

But apart from the contemplatives and the elderly who have made this passage, we will always have with us those who defy the necessity of making such a transition. These are the ones who have never known self-consciousness, and therefore have never known what it is *not* to see. I speak now of those who, by birth, accident, or disease, are considered mentally handicapped, and in particular I think of my niece who was born severely retarded. Long ago her mother assured me that little Marge never developed any concept of a self or of the other, and had never developed an affective system such as we know it. Watching her sit contentedly for hours, as if she were an outside observer on the mysterious world of the self-conscious, I used to wonder what she might be seeing and knowing that made it possible for her to stay in such a satisfied, peaceful state of mind. But like others who live in this unself-conscious state — infants, little children, a variety of individuals — she cannot tell us. Without first having had the relative experience of self-consciousness, there is no way to describe or communicate this non-relative type of seeing and knowing. It seems that wherever this state occurs, it is wrapped in silence; and even when it is communicated — as only the contemplative can do — it is rarely understood. Truly, it defies any form of intellectualization.

Since a large segment of society lives in this unself-conscious condition without being able to communicate it, the contemplative stands in a unique position to make an accounting for those who cannot do so. And in telling us something of this state, there is the revelation of the Creator's goodness, who has given the little ones to see "that" which the contemplative spends his whole life searching for and, literally, would give his eyetooth to see. Such a divine dispensation is no more mysterious than Christ promising heaven to the criminal on the cross — a common criminal who, for all we know, may have spent his entire life deriding God and hating his neighbor.

For those who have eyes to see, there is no place to

look where this Goodness is not revealed. This is the un-questioned object — indeed, the very subject — of the con-templative vision. In this way, he makes an accounting of this goodness, not for himself alone, but for those who can-not tell us what they see beyond a self-conscious condition. To me, the contemplative's sole function in society is to shed light on this dimension beyond the self, and to tell us about the crossing over, which is a journey few can talk about, but a journey which many are destined to make.

O

Although the final establishment in a state of union is an unmistakable transition in itself, it nevertheless lacks the finality, the definitiveness, and the abruptness of this second movement, wherein the union of two gives way to reveal the clear identity of the One. Here, the "who" of God and self have given place to the "what" of That which remains when they are gone. Thus, the glimpses of a complete loss of self, described by both St. Teresa and St. John of the Cross as merely "transient" (which somehow they did not foresee as a lasting state) have become a permanent reality, a reality of yet another step in the Eternal Movement.

The only mystic I could find who speaks of this step beyond union, beyond self and God, is Meister Eckhart. This is his "breakthrough," his "bursting forth" into the Godhead, his "crashing through to that which is beyond the idea of God and truth, until it (the soul) reaches the *in prin-cipio*, the beginning of beginnings, the origin or source of all goodness and truth" (R. B. Blakney, *Meister Eckhart*, Harper & Row, p. 169).

I regard this breakthrough as the beginning of the sec-ond contemplative movement, because the findings that lie beyond these landmarks — the falling away of the self and Eckhart's breakthrough — have much in common. Though it would be possible to spend the remainder of these pages pointing out their similarities, I shall content myself with a single quotation from the master:

> "When I flowed out from God, all things spoke: God is. But this cannot make me happy, for it makes me understand that I am a creature. In the breakthrough, on the other hand, where I stand free of my own will and of the will of God and of all his works and of God himself, there I am above all creatures and am neither God nor creature. Rather, I am what I was and what I shall remain now and forever....In this breakthrough I discover that I and God are one. There I am what I was, and I grow neither smaller nor bigger, for there I am an immovable cause that moves all things. Here, then, God finds no place in people, for people achieve with this poverty what they were in eternity and will remain forever." (Matthew Fox, O.P. *Breakthrough* Meister Eckhart's Creation Spirituality in New Translation, Image Books, p. 218)

As I read Eckhart, I read of one who has made the journey and crossed over. Yet, I also understand he was so outspoken about what he learned beyond the breakthrough that he eventually incurred the official censure of the Church. Apparently a few theologians were wary lest the common people — to whom he preached — might take him seriously and believe him when he talked of man's *essential* oneness with God, since this is, after all, a theological taboo. Despite his censure, however, it says much for theology that Eckhart, a theologian, never saw anything in his teaching contrary to the doctrines of the Church. On the contrary, he was certain that on an experiential or practical level he had only penetrated the Truth which theology attempts to define. Eckhart picked up, so to speak, where his Dominican brother left off when he not only expanded, but became eloquent, in the areas where St. Thomas had only fallen silent. Together, these two contemporaries have elaborated a contemplative system that ever remains incomplete if studied separately, or if this study is terminated with the more speculative of the two.

It is regrettable that, owing to this, the Spanish mystics found it necessary to bring the descriptions of their experiences into conformity solely with the speculative (Thomistic) aspects of the contemplative life. In doing so, the Eckhartian dimension beyond union was lost and therefore, remains unaccounted for in their writings. As said before, the reason for this loss is that "what" it becomes possible to know beyond the breakthrough is considered theologically improper.

To speak of an "accidental" oneness with God (union) is orthodox; but to speak of an "essential" oneness with God (identity) is considered unorthodox. And the problem is not merely one of description. Rather, it is primarily one of experience, for these are two different experiences: union before the breakthrough; identity, after the breakthrough. But this latter experience is not recognized because it does not harmonize with the theological insistence on an essential separation between Creator and creature. The creature in his union with God must always be "accidental" to God; and yet, in the experience of identity, the creature comes upon an "essential" union, which means partaking not only of God's is-ness, but of his what-ness.

Acknowledging this essential separation, Etienne Gilson asks the following question:

> What we want to know is simply this: whether, yes or no, we can admit the possibility of a coincidence, even partial, between the human substance and the Divine substance — whether we can admit it to be then in fact realized.

His answer is this:

> If you lower, were it but for an instant and at any point, the barrier set up by the contingence of being between man and God, then you rob the Christian mystic

of his God, and you rob him therefore of his mysticism. He can do without any god who is not inaccessible; the sole God Who by nature is inaccessible is also the sole God he can in no wise do without. (Etienne Gilson, "Unitas Spiritus," *Understanding Mysticism*, Edited by R. Woods, O.P. Image Books, pp. 500-501)

This amounts to saying that union depends on separateness, and in this he is correct; but beyond the self this separateness no longer exists and thus, he is also correct in saying that identity of substance (essence, as I call it) between man and God robs the mystic of both his God and his mysticism. In truth, coming upon this identity is the end of all longing and desire for God, for union, or for any type of experience, because this identity is by its very nature the ending of the contemplative life — which is why it is the beginning of a new life. In a word, God has become eternally accessible.

As I see it, coming upon pure Being (God) belongs to childhood; to recognize this Being as the ground of our soul and of all that exists, belongs to adolescence; and to go beyond Being to realize that in essence, let alone in Being, God is all that exists, belongs to adulthood; and it is *this* maturity, that lies beyond the breakthrough. At least, this is how I read Eckhart.

The root of the problem seems to stem from the belated biblical statement (not mentioned in Genesis) that God made all things from nothing, and that the crux of the disagreement between theologian and mystic lies in the interpretation of this nothingness. Since absolute nothingness is incomprehensible to the mind, it falls, like the essence of God, into the realm of the unknown. That this unknown nothing is *not* God, is the particular insistence of the theologian; but that this unknowable nothing turns out to *be* God, is the final realization of the mystic. In other words, what flowed forth from God in the act of Creation was some unknowable aspect of Himself. Thus if we were created from nothing, it can only mean nothing *knowable* to the mind,

which is the truth, since God's essence is intellectually unknowable. Yet, understanding experientially how God works
becomes possible once we get beyond the breakthrough.

But once again, the problem is not merely one of biblical interpretation; more importantly, it is one of experience,
for there does indeed exist a theologically defined oneness or
union with God; and at the same time, there is also an unde-
finable mystical oneness or identity for which theology has
no words. The difference depends on which side of the
breakthrough we stand: whether the self remains, or
whether it is dead and buried in the Godhead — as Eckhart
puts it. Each side represents two different ways of seeing and
knowing, which for now, I can do no more to emphasize.

However we wish to interpret the nothingness from
which we were made, it remains impossible to make a sensible case for the magic-wand theory of creation, especially
when it isn't necessary. It is difficult to justify any speculation
that God did not make us from himself since this fact does
not make us God, does not limit God to matter or to this
universe, does not do away with creation, contingency, or
change anything at all; nor does it conflict with any relevant
Christian belief. (If any, only the notion of eternal damna-
tion might be affected, but who needs this one? Certainly
God doesn't!) The idea that creation is somehow "accidental" to God — which makes it little more than a scientific
chance — is an idea I find so absurd that I dare not belabor
the point another minute.

My interest in all this should not be difficult to understand. From the outset of this journey, I knew I had gone beyond the limits of the particular contemplative frame of reference outlined by the Spanish mystics. But I went on to
find in Eckhart this lost dimension beyond union and self.
Initially I had but a single book on the Master, but at the
end of the journey my friend, Father L, passed on to me a
list of sources and a number of articles on the mystic and his
theology. What I learned was that the areas where theology

is wont to reinterpret and correct Eckhart, are the very areas of this lost dimension; and it is precisely because he is out-spoken here, where theology becomes most sensitive, that Eckhart is unique and unlike any other Christian mystic. Thus, where some are wont to draw the line on Eckhart — or to keep him in line — that is the point where he breaks through. To keep him in line means to lose this dimension, to rob him of his uniqueness, and to cut short the contemplative experience for those who would follow.

In closing this account, I feel a beginning has been made by clearing the ground for much more that remains to be said. As stated initially, this writing stems from the failure to find this movement beyond self in the classical contemplative literature, and though I am no longer concerned for myself, I am concerned for those who may come to a similar end when they discover that their traditional path has suddenly disappeared. Having made this journey I now see, and see clearly, that a dimension unmistakably exists beyond anything that could be described as the self's union with God — be it called Spiritual Marriage, transforming union, or whatever the terminology one may care to use. For the contemplative to regard such a union as the final or ultimate consummation of his spiritual life is a grave mistake. He is setting his sight at a midway point which, I now see, is too low, too close-in, and too narrow. At this point he may even be so centered in God that he is still subject to the illusion of personal deification, wherein his only feat is to unwittingly shortchange God. Whenever possible, it is best to get beyond such a point, even when letting go means surrendering this union with all its experiences and ensuing qualities of strength, love, certitude, and personal energies; for as long as there is any feeling, knowledge, or inkling that a self remains, he has not gone far enough.

Of our own accord, we cannot cross the line into the unknown. Only God knows if we are ready for such a step; only he can take us across and see us through. Nevertheless, it is vitally important to realize that such a step exists, that others have taken it, and to be prepared so there will be no illusions about what lies beyond the self. For us to give our self to God is, as Eckhart says, to give Him absolutely nothing; but for God to take away the self, is for Him to take absolutely everything. Though John of the Cross stresses the giving, over the taking, and Meister Eckhart stresses the taking, over the giving, the fact remains that no matter how we evaluate this exchange, these are two different movements, two different contemplative experiences.

While reading this account, a friend made the rather droll remark, "It sounds to me like you lost your soul!" Now I had never thought of it this way, yet I liked the idea because I always regarded the soul as God's habitat, a kingdom in which God and self dwell as an unbeatable team; thus, to lose this soul — what could possibly be left? Certainly it would not be me — or you. So what does it mean to lose your soul? I think it means the death of God and the self, a descent into hell, and a resurrection on the third day. In heaven we do not speak of souls, we only speak of saints; thus there may be no souls in heaven. I don't know. But if to be a saint in the next life means losing your soul in this life, then it follows that we should all lose our souls. But isn't this what Christ would have us do — to lose this life (our souls) that we might have eternal life? In new translation this saying turns into: "He who brings himself to nought for me discovers who he is." To this I would add that in coming to nought he will not only discover who he is, but "what" he is, for in God these cannot be separated. *That* he is, *what* he is, *who* he is, *where* he is, in God these are One, and outside this One, nothing is.